To Lyn,

Hope you f

Domestic Abuse: Men Suffer Too

Very best wishes,

Domestic Abuse: Men Suffer Too

Jason Hanson

Jason Hanson Counselling

CONTENTS

Acknowledgements

Very rarely can we conceptualise the time and effort that has gone into a book when we simply read the finished product. Having read many books in the past, ordinarily I am so immersed in the story within, I spare little thought to the story behind it, the sacrifices which have been made, the hours of sleep which have been lost and the rollercoaster of emotions encountered. Those close to me will know this book has been almost 3 years in the making (although admittedly I did take some time out in 2019). This has comprised of research, reaching out to victims who would be happy to share their stories, transcribing interviews, exchanging ideas with my clinical supervisor, writing and re-writing drafts, and ultimately producing the final version.

One of the things I have found most difficult along the way is balancing writing the book with a full time Psychotherapy practice, co-writing a second book, writing for the local paper (which I ultimately stepped away from in 2020), but most importantly, being a father and a husband. Of course there have been many influences along the way, but there are a few I would like to give special mention to, who in some way have contributed to this book.

Perhaps the best place to start is the front cover, and the wonderful illustrations provided by **Kerrie Neill**. I approached Kerrie with some ideas, but couldn't imagine just how captivating the finished product would be. Kerrie has captured the very essence of the book and set the scene with a gripping yet harrowing tone. I would also like to thank friend and clinical supervisor **Eric (Ric) Hoskins** for not only his input, but his support when I have felt overwhelmed and in need of another perspective. Ric contributed to the chapter on sexual abuse and also very kindly allowed me to use one of his case studies. Ric, I value our supervision sessions as much as our friendship and thank you sincerely for sharing your knowledge and expertise. Thank you for providing the sense checks when I most needed them.

Sincere thanks goes to **Myk Valentine** who provided me with some very useful information and statistics around domestic abuse within the LGBT+ community. Myk was happy to share the research he had conducted, providing me with a more in depth insight into an area which is often overlooked. Myk, I am extremely grateful for your input and hope the book has been able to raise the awareness of domestic abuse both for and within the LGBT+ community.

I would also like to extend my sincerest gratitude to **John Winfield** for agreeing to proof read this book in preparation for its publication. John, I will forever remain extremely grateful for you taking on a task of such magnitude.

I would like to say a very special thank you to those who agreed to share their stories, in the process becoming such an important part of the book. Whilst the names contained within the case studies may have been changed to protect the identity of the individuals, the stories told are very real. I found the experience personally inspiring, yet incredibly emotional at the same time. To the family of **Johnny** (a victim of domestic abuse who tragically lost his life), from the bottom of my heart, thank you for sharing his story. I feel both humbled and privileged you would entrust me with such a personal and emotive experience and can only hope telling his story gives you some comfort.

Last but not least, I would like to offer my heartfelt gratitude to my wife **Lynsey**, who not only actively encouraged me every step of the way, but also accepted me spending many hours away from the house. Lynsey was also instrumental in the layout and formatting of the book, something I am extremely grateful for. Lynsey, I cannot thank you enough for looking after our wonderful daughter **Aisla** during the many days and nights I have spent immersed in this book, whilst still finding time to support me. You asked me what was next after this book...well I think I owe you and Aisla some time back! Thank you, I love you both.

Finally for all those who offered kind words of encouragement, for all those who have provided unwavering support, for those who were kind enough to share their stories with me and for everybody out there who has been a victim of domestic abuse...this book is for you.

Imagine if this...

Was this...

Would your perception change?

1

✺

Introducing abuse

Let's lay these and other misconceptions to rest as we explore male domestic abuse in detail.

"When I was physically abused, I received: Police[1] *drive by (death threat made), shelter and counselling. When my brother was physically abused by his gf, he received: laughter from a responding cop and an escort from his home".*

This was a tweet which appeared on my feed on the 11th January 2021 and I think perhaps encapsulates the rationale behind the writing of this book. The author was happy for me to use this (although requested anonymity), to try to highlight that challenges around male domestic abuse are multi-faceted.

There are questions around whether male domestic abuse is talked about enough and whether awareness is at the levels it could, or in fact should be. This book will take a step toward raising awareness in hope that more people will recognise early signs of being in an abusive relationship. Secondly, and something which is intrinsically linked with aspects of the above, is tackling the existing stigma, which sadly is not only evident in individuals, but also sometimes within institutions. If an individual who may have been subjected to domestic abuse is dismissed, ridiculed or castigated at the time of reporting the crime, there is a danger of the problem being repressed, potentially resulting in a reticence by victims to come forward. This in turn impacts the statistics, providing an inaccurate picture of the issue (I will discuss later why crimes reported may not accurately depict crimes committed).

The intention of this book is not to propagate an agenda which sees a decrease in the focus on female victims, rather to highlight the need for an increased focus on male victims, ultimately exploring whether a non-gendered approach in tackling domestic abuse is the way forward. If you feel by the end of your reading that there has been any attempt to trivialise domestic abuse on women, or that it has proposed in any way that we should lessen the focus on female victims, then it has failed in this message. Whilst this book aims to be informative, it is also important it draws attention to, and raises the profile of, male domestic abuse within society. However what is equally important is that it recognises the severity of domestic abuse as an act whether victims are male or female, and addresses the question of whether a more holistic approach is necessary in tackling the issue.

Domestic abuse is a heinous act which can have long lasting and far reaching consequences for the victims irrespective of sex and/or gender. The book will aim to address the misconception that when it comes to abuse, men are always the perpetrators, and women the victims. It will provide you with an insight into the different types of abuse and warning signs as well as ways in which to seek support. At the end you will get a very powerful, yet emotional insight into the world of abuse from the victim's perspective, through some real life stories told by victims. Also included will be a very emotive story from an individual who has been profoundly affected since her brother tragically lost his life, having been subjected to prolonged physical and emotional domestic abuse at the hands of his wife. For those who have never experienced domestic abuse, it will provide you with an insight into some of the areas in which you can be vigilant, not only for yourself, but for friends and loved ones. For those who have not been so fortunate, this book will hopefully give you some reassurance that you are not alone and there is support available, whilst recognising the courage and bravery victims of domestic abuse display every day, regardless of whether they report this or not.

Whilst this book has a focus on male domestic abuse, it contains a significant amount of generic information which allows it to be both informative and resourceful. So regardless of your gender or sex, I invite you all to accompany me on this journey as we explore in detail the seen and the unseen and the subtle and the obvious, in the world of domestic abuse.

If you were to look at its history, one could argue the main change we have seen within this subject area is society's perception. We have progressed from this being seen as a private affair, to it now being met by most with condemnation. Laws have now been implemented to protect victims and deter perpetrators with more severe consequences. As a further step, towards the end of 2015 it was announced that controlling or coercive behaviour was to become a crime and would carry up to 5 years imprisonment for anyone found guilty. Whilst it would not be a stretch to suggest that domestic abuse on women has been occurring for centuries in what some would argue has been historically a patriarchal society, tracing domestic abuse with male victims presents more of a challenge. Certainly here in the UK, you could point to the Alex Skeel case as something which arguably propelled male domestic abuse into the national media.

Alex's ex-partner was jailed in 2018 for grievous bodily harm with intent as well as controlling or coercive behaviour[2]. In addition to domestic violence, also evident was prolonged psychological abuse, highlighting that not all abuse is visible. Alex had been scolded, beaten with various objects, stabbed and even deprived of food over a period of several years, resulting in physical and emotional trauma. He was also isolated from his family, effectively making him completely dependent on the perpetrator, with little option for escape.

Sadly, this won't be the first time you have read of a situation like this and it more than likely won't be the last either. However even with this in mind, it is still difficult to trace when male domestic abuse first became prominent and began generating any sort of recognition.

For those who have never experienced domestic abuse in any form, try to think of a situation which has elicited feelings of angst; a situation of unpredictability, whether that be a mild disagreement or an inevitable path to confrontation; the shaking, the stomach cramps, the nausea – the physical symptoms usually synonymous with anxiety. Accompanying these may be psychological aspects; the worry, the fear, the uncertainty. This is when we quite often get into what is known as the fight or flight mode (a term first used by Walter Cannon to capture what he described as the 'acute stress response' of animals). Domestic abuse in any sense is an extremely serious and potentially damaging act, but as we will explore, abuse and the scarring it can leave, are not always physical.

The concept of fight or flight arguably holds significant relevance when it comes to situations involving domestic abuse. Effectively, what we mean by this is we either prepare for the confrontation or we retreat to avoid it at all costs. Many of us will have been in this situation on at least one occasion and whilst reactions can vary from person to person, it could generally be agreed these situations can be unpleasant and have the capacity to cause severe discomfort. So if possible many of us will try to avoid them right? Now imagine, the situation feels inevitable and unavoidable; imagine the amplification of the aforementioned feelings and emotions due to the fact this is a regular, not sporadic occurrence; imagine living with that fear daily, and having it affect your appetite, your motivation, your friendships, your sociability, your physical appearance, your enjoyment of life. This list is not exhaustive, nor is that fear of confrontation and the thoughts of what inevitably may accompany this. It's constant, it's profound, yet for some people, it becomes so ingrained that it appears as a natural and accepted part of their lives. When we detail it like this, we may naturally ask the question around why people would accept this as their normal. We may posit that we have individual choice and raise the question of who would actively choose to put themselves, or remain in, a situation which induced the sort of symptoms discussed above. The question is simple, yet the possible answers involve more thought provoking complexities, which we will now begin to address.

Domestic abuse is perhaps a more regular occurrence than you may think with estimates of around 2 million reported cases in the year ending March 2018. At this point you may be thinking that you have read about many cases of domestic abuse and that the case discussed at the very beginning of the book tragically contains nothing you haven't previously come across. So why has this particular example been highlighted? In this instance the perpetrator was female and the victim was male. For some readers this may be all too familiar, whether it is something experienced directly, or seen in a friend or loved one. For others, this may be a difficult concept to grasp. In pre-industrial society, there were definitive conjugal roles and men and women were viewed differently. Some argue we still live in a patriarchal society which is dominated by men. Some theorise that women are controlled through violence and men are innately angry. However, male domestic abuse occurs more often than some may realise, with figures from the Office for National Statistics (ONS) showing approximately 35% of all abuse reported to the police is done so by male victims[3].

In the year ending March of 2020, reports of domestic abuse had increased to 2.3m with approximately 32% of these being from men aged 16-74.[4]

As previously mentioned, one of the key focuses of this book is to create an informative narrative which can potentially help those who may be in domestically abusive relationships to become more aware and seek positive changes. However keep in mind the information contained within it may benefit those who are fortunate enough to have little or no direct experience of domestic abuse just as much. As you will see as we progress, many victims of domestically abusive relationships do not become aware of the nature of their relationship until they are reflecting retrospectively. The main reason for this is that some forms of abuse are very subtle. Gaslighting is an example of this, where the victim may begin to question their own sanity, feelings or instincts. This will be discussed in more detail later in the book. One of the key factors we need to highlight is that domestic abuse and domestic violence are not one in the same. Whilst domestic violence sits under the umbrella of domestic abuse, it is only one aspect of it. A good way to look at domestic abuse is by considering an iceberg. The visible part, equates to domestic violence, where the signs are evident. However under the surface lies another substantial part not openly on view, but vast all the same.

2009 saw the World Health Organisation (WHO) publish

their paper on promoting gender equality to prevent violence against women. The paper focuses on how gender inequalities within society contribute to domestic abuse. So effectively it theorises that there are certain societal expectations synonymous with men which lead to an increased tendency for them to exercise control over women and view them as subordinate. Sociological theory tells us that historically, specifically in pre-industrial society, within the household there was evidence to suggest that men were viewed as dominant and women as dependent. In 1901 the employment rate for women (not including work in the home, which was often overlooked) was around 31%[5]. The Institute for Fiscal Studies (IFS) determined that in 1975, 57% of women aged 25-54 were in paid employment, with this figure rising in 2017 to a record high of 78%[6].

Indeed women have previously married for security and would often take on the expressive role within the relationship, whereas a man's role would be more instrumental. Whilst we have already discussed how there are different views on gender positioning within society, this is beyond the scope of the book, however, viewpoints such as these put us in danger of a gendered approach which arguably detracts from the overall problem of abuse. Any approach which makes generalisations based on gender runs the risk of creating an inaccurate narrative of an abusive relationship.

We must consider relationships which are free of abuse, as well as those where women are perpetrators and men are victims (same sex as well as heterosexual relationships). In 2018, the Government launched the 'No Defence for Abuse' Domestic Abuse Strategy 2018-2023. It was reassuring to see that domestic abuse involving male victims was highlighted, as were some of the charities, developed with the sole purpose of supporting male victims. However, this has not always been the case, and the previous lack of recognition for male victims may explain the reticence of men to come forward to report domestic abuse. By this rationale, you could raise the question of whether the current statistics around male domestic abuse are an accurate reflection of the prevalence, as they will only account for the instances reported and subsequently recorded. Back in 2010 the government strategy entitled 'Our Call to End Violence against Women and Girls' was published. In a forward, the Home Secretary at the time had said the simple premise behind this strategy was that no woman should have to live in fear of violence and all girls should be able to grow up knowing they are safe and able to have a good start in life. This is something I am wholeheartedly in agreement with, however I would question whether men should be afforded that same right. As part of this initiative, Clare's law was introduced, which effectively gave women the right to know if their partner had any sort of violent past. They also created protection laws for female genital mutilation (FGM), something which has seen an increase in media coverage in more recent times. All of these initiatives are a step in the right direction for tackling domestic abuse, but I am left wondering...don't men suffer too?

2

∽

The statistics

"Facts are stubborn things, but statistics are pliable" – **Mark Twain**

"Numbers never lie, after all: they simply tell different stories depending on the math of the tellers" - **Luis Alberto Urrea**

It is worth noting statistics do not always accurately depict that which they are measuring. We will take crime, more specifically domestic abuse, as an example here, and explore the process which sees a criminal activity become part of a wider statistic. There are two key things which need to happen for this to occur:

Reporting the crime

Primarily the victim has to report the crime to give it any chance of being recorded. This in itself raises an interesting question; to what extent do men feel comfortable reporting a crime in which society more commonly views them as perpetrators as opposed to victims? In 2015 an individual from Lancashire was murdered by his wife, and according to his former partner, he had hidden the abuse because he felt embarrassed by it. This is just one of many examples, and sadly this man was not alone in being the victim of domestic abuse and feeling that social stigma prohibited him from speaking out. There are of course other reasons why people choose not to report domestic abuse, which are not necessarily attached to social stigma.

Effectively in any relationship (and indeed in many other situations), there are three choices available:

- You accept things the way they are
- You make changes
- You leave

You could argue abuse victims to an extent are faced with the same three options, however in some instances it is worth thinking about to what extent the latter two are viable options. Additionally, considering the very nature of abuse it is also worth raising the question of how much control an abuse victim may actually have over their situation. Experience would tell us there are all too many instances where the only option is simply accepting things the way they are; the inevitability of continuous abuse. As a Psychotherapist, I have worked with many individuals (both male and female), where this has been the case and they have remained in abusive relationships for years, something which has affected them profoundly.

Some men of course feel they are able to change the behaviour and subsequently the environment, without the help of any external authorities. We sometimes see this reaction from people who feel the abuse is transient and uncharacteristic; people who feel they are still in control of the situation and can make the necessary changes.

It is important to remember that in many cases the abuser is somebody to whom we may have a strong emotional attachment to, which leads us to question why somebody who we hold these feelings toward would deliberately inflict pain or suffering on us. Also, and perhaps most importantly, for a crime to be reported, an individual would have to be aware they were indeed the victim of a crime. Keep in mind not all abuse is tangible, and even when it is, it is not always accepted by the victim as being abusive behaviour. Being the recipient of broken bones, bruising or swelling could and often is, justified in a variety of ways by the victim, from the perpetrator simply having a bad day, to taking personal responsibility and feeling the attack was provoked and warranted. For the latter, victim blaming may play a pivotal role. We also find that boundaries are individually defined in a relationship, so what may be seen as a form of domestic abuse by many, may be accepted as a normal part of a relationship by some. Other reasons can include not wanting to accept that the relationship is abusive or having a genuine fear of the repercussions should we choose to acknowledge and highlight it. This last point in itself is interesting because once we acknowledge the existence of something like this, we can feel a pressure to do something about it. This can elicit extreme feelings of trepidation, which is why some people will be reluctant to acknowledge the abuse in the first place. Suddenly, by externalising it, we make it real.

We will discuss in later chapters the more surreptitious types of abuse in detail, however emotional, psychological and financial abuse can be some of the more diplomatic forms where victims may not realise they are in an abusive relationship. Often this may not be discovered until after the relationship has ended, if at all. This is something which was substantiated in some of the case studies, which you will be able to read at the end of this book. Several of the victims were unaware they were in an abusive relationship at the time, with one individual not realising the extent of the abuse until we talked through it in my interview with him.

So we have detailed several reasons why domestic abuse, may not be reported, and I invite you to keep these in mind as we venture through this chapter on statistics and explore the question of

'Is domestic abuse in men underrepresented in the national statistics?'

Recording the crime

This one is a little trickier and we will attempt to deal with it in a sensitive and respectful manner. The official guidelines for a crime to be recorded by the police are:

"A crime must be recorded as soon as possible after the person receiving the report is satisfied that it is more likely than not that a crime has been committed"
(Home Office counting rules for recorded crime)

We are faced with 2 key challenges here. Firstly, the stigma around male victims and female perpetrators (of course sometimes it is male on male abuse) which exists can raise enough reasonable doubt as to whether the offence happened the way it has been conveyed or even whether it actually happened at all. Secondly, it's discretionary. Whenever anything is subjective, reliant on individual discretion, it opens us up to personal bias or even a lack of knowledge and understanding around a specific subject area. There have been instances when a man has called the police on a female aggressor and the police have entered the property and automatically arrested the man. A senior lecturer at Teeside university conducted a piece of research with male abuse victims where one individual had recounted calling the police to report domestic abuse, only for them themselves to be arrested due to a counter allegation made by their partner upon police arrival[7].

Recording the crime is a key component in providing an accurate reflection of the severity of the situation. Put simply, not all crimes are recorded for a variety of reasons and once victims either have direct experience of not being taken seriously, or become aware of instances where others have had that very experience, it could make them hesitant to disclose any current or future abuse.

However, we need to appreciate that recording the crime of abuse is not always straightforward. For example, reporting to the police that your partner controls the money in the relationship and doesn't want you to work (financial abuse), may not be something they would be readily able to prove, and this would in turn affect whether or not it was recorded. This in itself may be one of the key reasons why domestic abuse per se is so under-reported.

In my time as a therapist, I have worked with many abuse victims, witnessing very different reactions from the client. In almost all instances, the journey experienced in which they explore the details of what happened, and realise the amount of time for which it occurred, is a painful and highly emotional one. Some have not wanted to believe they could be subjected to such abuse by somebody they have been in an intimate relationship with. Others did not want to accept it as they saw it as a personal failure and felt like they had allowed this to happen, which in their mind highlighted weakness. Some were simply not aware of the full extent of the abuse until they started to explore their relationship in the therapeutic setting. Regardless of their experiences, and the emotionally challenging journey they encountered exploring the abuse, I can tell you that not one client who I have worked with had reported the abuse at the time they were undertaking therapy with me.

However I have worked with people who have experienced high levels of anxiety and fear because somebody else has reported the abuse anonymously. In many cases I was the only person they had discussed the abuse with, suggesting they had been carrying this burden on their own for an extended period of time.

The next chapter will take a more in depth look into some of the reasons for male domestic abuse being under-reported, but for now, let's take a closer look at some of the key statistics.

A document produced by Mankind Initiative in 2018 stated that...

'Male victims (39%) are over three times as likely as women (12%) not to tell anyone about the partner abuse they are suffering from. Only 10% of male victims will tell the police (26% women), only 23% will tell a person in an official position (43% women) and only 11% (23% women) will tell a health professional'.[8]

Figures from the Crime Survey for England and Wales (2018) show little change in the prevalence of domestic abuse in recent years[9], however as discussed, we need to keep in mind that not all crimes are reported, so these figures may not be wholly representative of the situation. In the year ending March 2018, it was claimed by the Office for National Statistics (ONS) that an estimated 2 million adults aged 16 to 59 years had experienced domestic abuse in the preceding year (1.3 million women, 695,000 men).

The police recorded 599,549 domestic abuse-related crimes in the year ending March 2018, which ultimately highlighted an increase of 23% from the previous year **(Office for National Statistics – Domestic Abuse in England and Wales: year ending March 2018).** There is an argument, this in part owes to police forces improving their identification and recording of domestic abuse incidents as crimes. You could also argue there is less reluctance from victims to come forward, which in turn has led to higher levels of reporting for these crimes.

The police made 225,714 arrests for domestic abuse-related offences (keep in mind these statistics were supplied from the 39 forces who had the information readily available and were able to supply the data). This equates to 38 arrests per 100 domestic abuse-related crimes recorded. The percentage of convictions secured for domestic abuse-related prosecutions is at its highest level since the year ending March 2010. In the year ending March 2018, 76% of prosecutions resulted in a conviction **(Office for National Statistics – Domestic Abuse in England and Wales: year ending March 2018).**

However, whilst there is evidence of an increase in prosecutions, there are still many instances where cases of domestic abuse may not result in arrest or prosecution and this in itself may create an aversion to reporting the crime. It can take a tremendous amount of courage to disclose a crime, knowing there is a chance of the abuser being reprimanded and at least spoken to by the police. If this does not result in arrest, there may be a fear the victim has further antagonised the abuser, resulting in those feelings of anxiety being greatly exacerbated. Sadly, when it comes to male domestic abuse, there is also the risk that the victim may well be the one arrested, and for some this is a key consideration when determining whether they report the abuse or not.

It is also worth exploring how the statistics are actually recorded. For example, the crime survey for England and Wales is based around interviews with a small proportion of households with a purpose of trying to reach out to those who, for various reasons, may not have reported the crime to the police. Some of these involve face to face interviews, which in itself raises questions of validity. This technique can certainly induce trepidation and people may feel anxious disclosing to another individual in person. Alternatively, there are self-completing questionnaires, which can help to alleviate feelings of angst in respondents when answering questions of a more sensitive nature. Keep in mind the questionnaire, considering the subject, is likely to be highly emotive and this may prove challenging for an individual, in turn influencing how they complete it, if at all. Whether it is face to face or in written format, once those words have been externalised, the situation becomes real, and that process can be very difficult for somebody to overcome psychologically, to the extent they will avoid it at all costs.

There are two equally important factors we should also give consideration to here. Firstly, not everybody may be consciously aware that they are being subjected to domestic abuse. Remember, some of the signs will be on a spectrum which will see them ultimately determined by frequency. This then becomes subjective because that which may be considered by one to be infrequent, may be considered frequent to another. Unless there is definitive directive as to precisely what constitutes domestic abuse, figures will never be completely indicative of the situation. As discussed previously, some people may be in denial because the reality of what is actually happening may challenge their perception of their partner as well as their relationship, and this may be too painful for them to accept. The second key factor to consider is that when you are looking at these surveys, within their official definition of what constitutes domestic abuse, there is one key omission – 'controlling or coercive behaviour' (CCB).

As an addendum to the Serious Crimes Act, in 2015, the Government created a new offence known as 'controlling or coercive behaviour'[10]. (This necessitates further exploration and will be done so in its own chapter later in the book). Since the law's inception in December 2015, figures have highlighted an increase in controlling or coercive behaviour with reported cases rising from just under 5000 in 2016/17 (across 38 police forces) to circa 25,000 in 2019/20 (across 42 police forces). In each year approximately 93-94% of victims of CCB were female[11]. The figures suggest overwhelmingly that CCB is something which is predominantly propagated by men, however they don't necessarily reflect the whole picture and for various reasons many instances may go unreported (by both male and female victims). We will delve into this at a later juncture.

One of the deterrents for people reporting any type of abuse can be the relatively low prosecution rate. This is particularly evident within CCB cases and possibly provides an explanation as to why it may be something which is under-reported. In 35% of CCB offences in 2018/19, whilst the victim was advocating further action, there was a difficulty finding sufficient supporting evidence to prosecute, meaning no further action could be taken. As a result of this, only 6% of reported cases culminated in charges being brought against the perpetrator[12]. According to the Home office review (2021), prosecutions have steadily increased since the first year of the Act being introduced and in 2019/2020, some 1208 cases had been successfully prosecuted in relation to controlling or coercive behaviour.

Whilst there have been questions raised about gender bias, we have to be mindful that we may not have an accurate ratio of male to female victims when it comes to CCB. However it is important that male victims feel comfortable enough to come forward and disclose without the fear of conscious or unconscious bias. We do appear to be witnessing a change in the perception of domestic abuse on men, and it feels like with the stigma slowly beginning to reduce, coupled with more information now being circulated in society and the media, we are moving some way toward addressing this imbalance in attitudes. However there is an argument we are still some way off. So just how prominent is domestic abuse involving male victims?

If we begin in 2012, we see through official police reporting figures that 19% of reported crimes around abuse were from men. In 2017, this had increased to 23%, however it had peaked at 24% in the 2 previous years, which had seen a 5% rise in male victims reporting domestic abuse. It is also interesting to look at the geographical makeup of the reporting. In 2012 & 2013 Hampshire saw 37% & 39% of the total domestic abuse reports, filed by men. In 2017, in Hertfordshire, male reports of domestic abuse accounted for 42%, which is a staggering amount and may suggest that more men are now beginning to feel comfortable reporting being involved in a domestically abusive relationship.[13]

Whilst some of these figures highlight a rise in the reporting of domestic abuse, holistically there still exists a challenge within this area. It is estimated that a higher percentage of men consider taking their own lives due to partner abuse than women (11% & 7.2% respectively). In addition to this, and something which has been synonymous with men speaking about their own mental health, the amount of men who will disclose abuse to another person is worryingly decreasing. In 2017/18 it was thought that nearly 2/3 of men would not disclose being victims of domestic abuse[14].

For some of the reasons outlined in this chapter (which we will explore in more depth in the next), it is difficult, as with domestic abuse in general, to ascertain precise figures for the prevalence of male domestic abuse. What we mean by this is that many of the figures available highlight the number of people who may have been victims, however what they do not tell us, is how often that abuse has occurred. So are these single instances or more indicative of prolonged abuse? To elaborate on this, whilst we have one figure for those who have reported being victims of abuse, the figure relating to actual instances, will undoubtedly be significantly higher. Single instances may represent the largest proportion of incidents of domestic abuse which are not reported. One of the key reasons for this is that we often view abuse as something which is recurring and may attribute a single incident to something else. This provides us with an ongoing challenge in obtaining data which accurately reflects the problem in society, with some people simply unaware they have been the victim of domestic abuse. Therefore the statistics we have available to us are only an approximation of the size of the problem.

3

Why is male domestic abuse under-reported?

"Men are supposed to be strong, who is going to believe me?"

The most up to date statistics (at the time of writing) relating to reported domestic abuse come from the ONS and cover the year ending March 2020. If we look back at recent government strategies, they have been predominantly focused on women, which means male domestic abuse may have been in the shadows.

It is vital we acknowledge that these strategies are both needed and welcomed by those wishing to see a reduction in prevalence, and an increase in awareness and convictions. However, it is equally important to recognise that in a society where approximately 1/3 of reported domestic abuse incidents come from male victims, government strategies should perhaps be reflecting the wider problem as opposed to being gender specific.

In December 2015 the Minister for Preventing Abuse and Exploitation, Karen Bradley, was speaking about the new measures which were to come into force to tackle the issue of controlling or coercive behaviour. Of course this was a welcome development in tackling domestic abuse, however you could argue it did little to address the perception within society that abuse victims are indeed on the whole female. She was quoted as saying...

"No one should live in fear of domestic abuse, which is why this government has made ending violence against women and girls a priority"[15].

In March 2016, then Home Secretary, Theresa May, published the VAWG[16] strategy, committing to tackling the issue of specifically, domestic violence against women and girls. Shining the spotlight on domestic violence, highlighting strategies to tackle the issue was generally seen as a positive move. However, this felt like a missed opportunity to tackle domestic abuse on a wider level, instead placing the focus on a more gendered approach. The problem with this is not only does it overlook male victims, but it also further propagates the notion that domestic abuse is synonymous with male perpetrators and female victims, something which ultimately heightens the stigma and arguably acts as a barrier to some men speaking out about their abuse.

Could these initiatives inadvertently contribute to the popular belief that domestic abuse and violence really only affects women? Is there an argument they run the risk of creating division rather than solidarity?

In September 2010, the Guardian published an article claiming that 40% of all domestic abuse involved a male victim based on research by the charity 'Parity' who felt that male domestic abuse was being ignored by the police and media[17]. Fast forward 9 years and we see, thanks to dedicated work by campaigners and charities, the government have developed a strategy aimed at supporting male domestic abuse victims.

On the proposal, Minister for Crime, Safeguarding and Vulnerabilities, Victoria Atkins (speaking in March 2019) said:

"Men can, and do, suffer from crimes such as domestic and sexual abuse. It is a horrendous experience that often goes unrecognised and it is heartbreaking some men feel they cannot report their experiences because of societal views around masculinity."[18]

At the beginning of this book we addressed the figures and explored whether or not the official statistics are an accurate depiction of the issue. We have to keep in mind that not all crime is reported and of those which are, sometimes we are relying on a judgment call from the individual who received the report as to whether they feel there is validity in the complaint, which will therefore determine whether it will indeed be recorded as a crime or not. However, this only highlights the issue of the prevalence of male domestic abuse and there is another important question we must ask, which precedes the recording of the crime: Is male domestic abuse under-reported, and if so why?

If you discuss the subject of domestic abuse with people, you will more often than not hear some reference to physical violence. There is an argument that the perception of abuse being primarily synonymous with physical violence specifically with a male aggressor and a female victim is part of the problem as it detracts from the other forms of serious abuse. As will be explored in greater detail in subsequent chapters, there are various forms of abuse and whilst violence can leave tangible markings, other forms conceal the evidence, making it more difficult to detect and prosecute. By this very rationale we discover there exists more subtle types, to the extent where there are many people who may be unaware they are being subjected to abusive behaviour. Therefore, it is a safe assumption that people will not report a crime they are unaware is actually taking place.

A recent article from the BBC in which they interviewed a domestic abuse victim highlighted one of the reasons why victims are wary of coming forward and reporting domestic abuse. In it, the individual disclosed they were subjected to 'nasty' behaviour and attacked in their sleep, which became more regular over time. [19]

"I couldn't do anything other than try and hold her off. It was very difficult; you are judged by people like the police as if you were the one who was causing everything. They don't understand men are getting abused, though I think they're starting to."

The media and society's expectations

It's a sad indictment on our society that due to societal perceptions and gender expectations people will invariably suffer in silence. It is difficult and distressing to believe that some people feel it is a better option to be subjected to domestic abuse by a partner over a prolonged period of time, rather than risk the reaction and judgment of society and the authorities.

This perhaps highlights the need for more awareness around the profoundly negative effects being in an abusive relationship can have on an individual. It's important to acknowledge that the effects on a person can be lasting and something which may impact future relationships. When we work with individuals in the therapeutic setting and they are presenting with challenges in their relationships, it is not uncommon to find after exploration that some of their behaviours and trepidations within their current relationship, can be traced back to things they experienced in a previous one. Naturally, we can be governed by past experiences and traumas.

You could argue the media have, certainly in the past, played a role in the public perception of domestic abuse. Much of what we have seen or read has centred round women as victims and men as perpetrators. From a cognitive perspective, this repeated exposure normalises domestic abuse as part of our society. There is an argument to an extent that we almost become desensitised to it. So when the repeated exposure predominantly conveys men as perpetrators, that becomes the norm and sets society's expectations. By this rationale, you can see why some people feel it is a difficult battle to change society's gendered view of domestic abuse.

If you want to understand a little more about society's perception relating to this subject area, then consider this:

At the time of writing, it was discovered in an experiment that if you conduct a Google search simply typing "reasons why people do not report domestic abuse", out of your first 7 hits, 4 of them will contain '*domestic violence*' and 3 of them will include '*women*', in their synopses.

To reiterate, the purpose of this book is not to detract from domestic abuse on women, more to highlight that whilst prevalence in accordance with official statistics suggests women are more likely victims, they are not the sole victims. A continued gendered approach is only going to add to the existing stigma and dissuade male victims from coming forward and speaking out. Across the globe, if you take a look at the statistics around murder, you will see that the victim pool is heavily weighted towards men. However we hear very little about murder being a gendered crime, so I question why this is so different when it comes to looking at domestic abuse. When there are charities that propagate the message that physical abuse and violence is much more severe when perpetrated by a man as opposed to a woman, it promotes a very dangerous rhetoric and does nothing to address an already existing stigma. During the writing of this book I was contacted by a lady who had lost her brother to domestic abuse at the hands of a woman. Her message was powerful and thought provoking, and she was actively campaigning to gain more recognition for male domestic abuse. Throughout this book tragically, you will see other examples of extremely violent abuse from a woman towards a man, which has ended up in either serious injury and emotional scarring or tragically, the loss of life. This is not about diminishing or trying to lessen the importance of one cause, it's about highlighting another. Moving forward, it would be more fruitful for charities to galvanise and provide a united front in tackling a shared cause under the umbrella of domestic abuse, rather than targeting genders independently.

The emotional attachment

Another key reason as to why domestic abuse is under-reported is found in the emotional attachment that we form to partners. Sometimes it is difficult to accept that somebody you love and care for, and perhaps have done so for a long period of time, could deliberately inflict harm upon you; could exhibit behaviour with the intention of eliciting feelings of sadness and despondency within you; could show a disregard for your emotional and physical well-being; or quite simply isn't the person you thought they were. The process in which somebody arrives at that realisation can be a difficult and sometimes elongated one. It can be extremely hurtful to accept you had invested your time and love into somebody, given yourself to them physically and emotionally, only to be treated in this manner. Even when people do come to that realisation, we must consider that there may well be strong feelings and emotions attached to the individual, and whilst moving away from the relationship is one thing, seeing a partner reprimanded and consequently punished is something very different.

In 1973 a bank robbery took place in Stockholm, Sweden which saw 4 hostages held in a vault for more than 130 hours[20]. Once the siege had come to an end, it transpired that the hostages had formed an unlikely bond with their captors, to the extent that they had refused to testify against them in court. This was the birth of what became clinically known as 'Stockholm Syndrome', which relates to captives forming irrational bonds with their captors. Over the years there have been examples of people developing bonds and attachments with captors to varying degrees. Stockholm syndrome has 3 key characteristics:

- The victim may develop positive or sympathetic feelings towards their captor or the person abusing them.
- The victim may take on a more negative view of those who may be trying to help them or reprimand their captor, sometimes to an extent they will refuse to cooperate.
- The victim identifies with their abuser, believing they have the same values and goals.

It is not wholly uncommon to see Stockholm Syndrome (whether in part or in its entirety) manifest itself within abusive relationships. Abuse can last for many years, and due to the controlling element which is often evident, abusers are able to perpetrate 2 types of behaviour which could explain Stockholm syndrome. Firstly it is important to remember that not all abuse is apparent and many victims may not in fact be aware they are victims of abuse at the time. This can see abusers use a mixture of occasional humility in and amongst subtle abusive techniques. Due to these actions being sometimes clandestine, the victim may only see the (perceived) periodic bouts of kindness. As a result, they can find it difficult to accept if faced with the reality of the abuse because their focus has solely been on any perceived positive gestures. Secondly, one of the ways an abuser will control somebody is by creating a dependency. Effectively what we see here is somebody following a sequence of behaviours and actions to isolate the individual. They will do this by firstly creating frictions between the individual and family or friends, convincing them that they (the family or friends) do not care and it is in fact they (the abuser) who hold their best interests. Secondly they will try to assert pressure on the individual to move away from others and forge a life solely with them. Once this has been achieved one of two things can happen. Either the abuser establishes themselves as the 'saviour' providing comfort whenever the other person is upset. The paradox of this of course is that most often it is the abuser who has caused the upset in the first instance. This can slowly develop into a pattern which makes it harder for the individual due to having a lack of options for support because they have been alienated. They have at this point quite possibly become completely reliant on the abuser. The other method which is common is to slowly emotionally abuse an individual to such an extent that they feel hopeless or lost without the abuser. I have worked with abuse victims in the past who have very much been subjected to this and were left to feel that nobody else would love or support them and therefore remaining with the abuser was seen as preferable to the alternative of feeling completely alone and unable to cope.

Some people feel they will not be taken seriously by authorities or worse still, reprimanded themselves; some fear the repercussions of reporting an abusive partner; some feel society does not view men as victims; others have formed an emotional attachment to the abuser and in their mind do not wish to jeopardise this. Regardless of the reasoning, the fact is that male domestic abuse remains under-reported and one of the battles we must face when tackling this is doing everything humanly possible to remove the barriers which may be preventing victims from disclosing.

4

Physical abuse

"It was just a slap...and he deserved it"

"It was a one off; I don't usually lose my temper like that"

"The cuts, the bruises, the scratches, the burns...I'm running out of excuses to tell people when I can't conceal the evidence"

Ask many about domestic abuse and you will most likely hear some reference to physical violence. Whilst there are several other forms of domestic abuse, historically, violence was the one most synonymous with the term. However, you could argue other forms of abuse have always existed, we just didn't recognise them as being symptoms of abusive behaviour until more recently. A good example of this would be the Serious Crimes Act of 2015 (introduced and referenced earlier in the book), which highlighted for the first time, that controlling or coercive behaviour is a crime and would be punishable by law. The main thing to consider about why physical abuse is arguably the crime (relating to domestic abuse) which contains the most convictions, is that it can be easier to prove and therefore investigate. What we mean by this is there is tangible evidence which can be examined. Other forms of domestic abuse are not so obvious (although one could argue the manifestation of psychological effects certainly are). This means essentially, we are placing more of an emphasis on raising awareness so individuals who are potentially being subjected to one of the subtler forms of domestic abuse, can feel empowered to take action knowing there is help available.

If we explore the statistics, we find that domestic violence still dominates the police recorded crime in relation to domestic abuse related offences. In the year ending March 2018, the offences recorded across England and Wales which were identified by police as involving domestic abuse, were circa 600,000. Just short of 459,000 of these were recorded as containing violence against the individual[21].

How do we specifically define what physical domestic abuse is though? Domestic violence can manifest itself in a multitude of ways including, punching, biting, slapping, kicking, striking with an object, burning, cutting – really anything which exerts unwanted and harmful physical force over another individual. It is often used as a way of undermining or controlling. Put simply, domestic violence can be used as a method to maintain control over an intimate partner. You could also argue that things such as forcing somebody into drugs or soliciting, or deliberately withholding medication from them, could also be seen as an act of physical abuse.

In the year ending March 2018, according to the Office for National Statistics, just over 25% of domestic abuse related offences which contained violence against the person, contained male victims[22]. Whilst we would ordinarily associate domestic violence victims as being within the younger generation, it is worth noting that the age group of 60-74 year-old men have been found to be particularly vulnerable[23].

Again, if you research domestic violence, you will find the majority of articles are dedicated to supporting female victims. Whilst there are some charities and organisations who do offer support specifically to men, sadly, they are still very much underrepresented. Domestic violence has been vilified for several decades now with the first battered women's shelter opening in 1971 in the UK. However, what is perhaps quite alarming, is that despite in a 1996 crime survey an equal proportion of men and women openly disclosing they had been subjected to physical abuse from a partner in the previous year; and with one third of all of those instances containing injury involving male victims, it was not until 2003, that the first shelter for battered men was to open[24]. Whilst the number of shelters for battered men is not in proportion with the percentage of male victims across the UK, the picture in London is bleaker still. An article by the Evening Standard in August 2018, stated that despite on average 150,000 calls to the police from male domestic abuse victims per year, there is not one single shelter for battered men in the London borough[25]. I was interested to recently read a briefing from the chairman of Mankind Initiative which had been written in 2016. At that time (according to the briefing), despite circa 500,000 men suffering from partner abuse, there were only 19 organisations which offer refuge or safe house facilities for victims. This translates to 78 spaces, however if you break this down further to only include those specifically open to men, the figure decreases significantly to just 20 places[26]. The same report also concludes that out of the 100 people who died at the hands of their partner between 2014-2015, 19% of these were men.

You only have to look at literature and media coverage to ascertain that violence within relationships is often conveyed as having a male aggressor and a female victim. This along with societal definitions around conjugal roles within the family and society in general, can make it extremely difficult for men to come forward and report. In addition to this, the proportion of domestic abuse crimes reported by men, to the amount of perpetrators charged, is very low.

In 2009, the World Health Organisation published a document which aimed to promote gender equality to prevent violence against women.

Whilst I applaud any initiative which addresses domestic abuse, there is an argument that the grasp of gender based violence here fails to take into consideration other contributing factors, omitting male victims with female aggressors and female victims with female aggressors. The very title of the report makes inferences only to the need for gender equality to address the violence towards women by men. I find myself recognising a certain paradox in promoting gender equality in society, whilst at the same time not extending this equality to the domestic abuse sphere. Of course there is an argument that traditional views of gender roles within society can lead to in some instances, male dominated and patriarchal households or relationships, a concept certainly propagated by feminist movements. This issue is still evident in pockets of society and certainly not something I would dispute. Highlighting the experience of male victims does not serve to dismiss or undermine this. I would certainly never detract from any form of abuse or oppression experienced by women in society, but we do need to realise that men can, and do, suffer too, whether at the hands of a woman or another man. Addressing gender inequality and perceptions of the gender roles in society may help to address domestic abuse towards women, however I am left questioning what is required to address the issue of male domestic abuse.

Physical abuse or anger will ordinarily come from one of 3 things; pain, fear or frustration. Sometimes more than one of these may be noticeable concurrently. Whilst there is a need to understand the reasons behind this form of abuse, it is equally important to acknowledge that reason does not translate to justification in terms of prolonged domestic abuse. In 2016 the Guardian published an article highlighting a domestic abuse case where tragically a 51 year-old man had lost his life just weeks after his wedding day[27]. He had been regularly beaten and left with black eyes and broken ribs as well as cuts and bruises. According to somebody who knew him personally, he had stated he would not be allowed to leave and felt embarrassed by what was happening to him. Social stigma seems to be the main reason that men do not seem to come forward with cases of domestic abuse, particularly when it comes to the more physical side. This may be attributed to societal perceptions which tell us that men are the stronger sex and should not be in a position where they are physically vulnerable. This perception seems to be further compounded by the fact that as of 2011, whilst there were approximately 4000 refuge centres for women, for men there were just 16. Perhaps this in itself is indicative of how prevalent male domestic abuse is in the eyes of wider society.

One of the debates around the different forms of abuse is how we actually categorise them. Some will put sexual abuse in its own category for example, while others feel sexual abuse should be contained within the category of physical abuse or even under coercion or control. We will cover sexual abuse briefly here, but it is certainly something which necessitates its own chapter at a later juncture.

When we consider domestic abuse, I wonder how often people are so preoccupied with the thought of physical violence that they negate to consider other forms of physical abuse such as rape? When it comes to male victims, it is perhaps easy to see why this is overlooked and not readily recognised or acknowledged. Whilst you can trace recognition of female rape back several centuries, you only have to go back to 1994 to find when male rape was first recognised. In 2003, it was then determined by law that rape victims were considered to be gender neutral meaning that the focus was on the parts of the body which were penetrated against the individual's will as opposed to the gender of that person. However as we will discover later, there are controversies around the terms and definitions of crimes of a sexual nature as well as a lack of parity regarding punishments associated with any such offences. This perhaps offers an insight into how the genders were perceived throughout society and may also give us an explanation as to why men are so reticent to come forward to report rape or sexual assault. Somehow it doesn't feel like 27 years is a long time to overcome centuries of attitudes and perceptions around men and women in our society. Let's look at some statistics to see whether post 2003 has seen more male rape cases reported. Keep in mind that statistics may not be a wholly accurate reflection of the issue due to the clear distinction we must draw between crime committed and crime reported. The Crown Prosecution Service (CPS) published data in 2015/2016 which highlighted 608 male rape victims, however this figure may not be wholly representative as a further 1734 rape victims did not have their gender recorded[28]. The same report concluded that 16% of domestic abuse victims were men. What these statistics have highlighted is a shift in focus and attitude when it comes to recognising and supporting male domestic abuse victims. In September 2017, the Government announced a new initiative designed to provide more support for male victims of rape, domestic abuse and sexual abuse. The aspiration with this new initiative was to remove some of the barriers that male abuse victims encounter which can prohibit or dissuade them from reporting abuse. Interestingly the same report produced findings that state that boys are more likely to be abused by authority figures, yet still much of the focus in previous years has been on girls and women[29].

When we discuss sexual violence, it is important we widen the scope and move beyond rape. Sexual violence is when somebody is forced into any unwanted sexual act, which can also include sexual harassment. In March 2017, the Crime Survey for England and Wales (CSEW) estimated that around 631,000 males had been subjected to sexual violence since the age of 16, with approximately 138,000 aged 16-59 having experienced an assault in the preceding year.[30]

Perhaps the most alarming statistic around sexual violence came from a 2013 report titled '*An overview of Sexual Offending in England and Wales*'[31]. This identified that only around 15% of individuals who were subjected to sexual violence reported it to the police. The report also concluded that in around 90% of the cases, the perpetrator will be known to the victim, whether this is a family member, friend, acquaintance, colleague or even an intimate partner. The aforementioned report makes very interesting reading and will be linked in the reference section at the end of this book should you wish to explore it in more depth.

As we have discussed previously, it is important we keep 2 key factors in mind when exploring statistics. Firstly we are reliant on the individual reporting the crime. There are numerous reasons why this may not happen and the statistics above support the notion that any figures we possess may simply be an estimate and not an accurate reflection. Secondly, and this also underpins one of the key messages of this book, a prerequisite for reporting a crime, is being aware a crime is actually being committed. Within any relationship, boundaries and expectations will be individually defined. If the relationship involves control or coercion, then it is likely that the sexual abuse has been normalised and the victim does not even realise that they are in fact a victim. Without this re-alisation, there is little chance of the crime being reported.

As an addendum, it is not uncommon for people within a re-lationship to justify their behaviour by attributing it to having a high sex drive and making their partner feel that they have a right to partake in sexual activity whenever they choose to as this is part of being in a relationship.

Whether it is through fear or a lack of recognition around the situation an individual finds themselves in, the enormity of the problem cannot be fully comprehended until there is more aware-ness, more support and fewer stigmas attached to male domestic abuse.

Perhaps one of the least covered and arguably most sensitive forms of male domestic abuse, centres round cultural occurrences. When it comes to physical violence, men and adolescents can also be the victims of forced marriage and honour-based violence, how-ever this again feels very much under-reported. This is an area which has perhaps almost flown under the radar, despite research suggesting that 20% of honour-based violence victims are in fact male[32]. Whilst male victims of honour-based violence face sim-ilar social stigma, there are other factors which can also play an important role in their decision not to report this. Primarily there can be a very real fear of repercussions. Honour-based violence is often about shame or unwanted attention being brought upon a family. There have sadly been many instances of children losing their lives for such reasons, which can often act as a deterrent from people reporting such cases. Victims may feel like reporting the crime brings further shame upon their family and their stand-ing within the community and may be genuinely fearful of their lives should this happen. So for many victims, where we discussed the 3 options at the beginning of the book, in their mind there is only 1, and that is to accept what is happening. The statistics for honour based violence are vague and for many reasons, do not represent the full scale of the occurrences. There were 2,600 cases of honour-based violence (including forced marriage and FGM) recorded by 41 out of 43 police forces between March 2014 and January 2015. 200 honour-based violence-related offences were referred by police to the CPS in 2016/17 (136 defendants charged).[33] Perhaps the key thing to note here again, is how gendered these reports appear to be, with little reference to honour-based violence against men. It is due to factors like these, as well as some of those mentioned above why we see so few male victims of such violence report the abuse. Accepting that you are in an abusive relationship can be difficult, speaking out and taking strides to remove yourself from that abusive environment, even more so. The fear of physical violence is something which probably resonates with most people, however for some it is a much more real threat. Imagine being in a situation where you are subjected to prolonged violence, but have such trepidation about the alternative, that this becomes the lesser of 2 evils and is essentially normalised. This is not something anybody should have to live with and it is imperative we continue to promote the message that physical abuse is not mono gendered.

5

~

Emotional and psychological abuse

"It's not abuse;
I've never laid a
hand on him"

"It's just a bit of
fun, he needs to
lighten up"

"They say it's just banter, but it doesn't feel like that to me. I have no confidence and feel hopeless"

Whilst we may be able to hide physical scars, there are often signs that somebody is being subjected to physical violence. Psychological or emotional abuse by comparison can be more difficult to detect. There is no concealing a physical attack, but what happens when abuse is less noticeable? What happens when there may be no tangible evidence that we are in fact victims of abusive behaviour? When we look at emotional or psychological abuse we are faced with a certain ambiguity, largely due to the fact there are numerous methods abusers may employ which can make it more difficult to recognise. Whether the abuse is subtle, or whether there is a lack of awareness around what constitutes abusive behaviour, some people will inevitably be victims without realising. One of the key questions which accompanies this is how we distinguish between somebody who is unkind in the moment, and somebody who is deliberately abusive.

One argument is when it is prolonged and consistent it begins to enter the realms of emotional abuse. The problem with using this definition however, is that it negates to consider single acts, which can have long and far reaching emotional consequences for an individual. I came across this quite recently in practice, where a client had been told suddenly that he was not the biological father of his children.

The effects of this were significant enough for the individual to seek therapy to try to understand how to process this. Whether or not he was the biological father of the children (something which was not established through his therapy), this was an example of emotional abuse which was clearly designed to cause emotional unrest and place doubt within the individual. To understand just how severe emotional abuse can be, we can explore the impact this had on the client. The initial reaction to this was one of shock and distress, shortly followed by a period of extreme despondency. These were influenced by 3 thoughts. Firstly, what if the children he had loved and raised through the years were not his and the bond he had forged with them had been built on deception? Secondly, how could somebody who was close to him say something so hurtful, irrespective of its validity? Finally he raised the question of the impact this may have on the children. What if he were to consciously or unconsciously behave differently toward them now? How would that bond with them be affected? Accompanying this was of course the anxiety, the fear about the future and how he could move forward if his children were indeed not biologically his. Then there was the breakdown in trust with his wife, but also a questioning of others around him. If there was truth in this, how many others had known and willingly kept it from him? The lack of trust then escalated and he found himself withdrawing from friends, family and work colleagues as a result.

During therapy he began casting doubts on many of his platonic relationships, which exacerbated the low moods and in turn the anxiety...One small comment.

Whilst there is little subtlety in physical violence, emotional abuse can be much more calculated and diplomatic, but often leaving scars more severe. Physical scars symbolise effect, the end product, but the reason emotional scars are argued to be more severe is because they symbolise the reasons sat behind the attack. Physical scars in most cases will cease hurting us at some point, but their presence may always act as a painful reminder, and the accompanying pain and anguish can be much more difficult to process. Sometimes people will self-harm so they have a physical representation of their emotional pain.

When we research into the different existing forms of abuse, it is not uncommon to see a difference of opinion. When it comes to **emotional** and **psychological** abuse, you will find some who will draw clear distinction whilst others view them as one and the same. Whilst psychological abuse is something which can affect our thoughts, the effects of emotional abuse are focused more around how we feel. I will cover them both under the same chapter, as whilst you can see some subtle differences, there are also similarities between the two. Emotional or psychological abuse has many facets to it, some which may be quite easy to identify, others not so much.

For example if somebody shouts at you causing you to feel intimidated, this is noticeable behaviour which is deemed to be abusive and unacceptable. Often we see this type of behaviour displayed as an attempt to exert control over another individual; to make them feel small, intimidated and unable to defend themselves. Whilst it may feel like it carries less of an impact than physical abuse, this can leave people feeling helpless and reluctant to offer their opinion in any given situation as their confidence has been eroded. It can promote an acceptance that irrespective of how something may affect you, it is not fruitful to voice how you are feeling, as this will inevitably escalate into an extremely unpleasant situation. Emotional abuse can also create a reliance and co-dependency. What we mean by this is that an individual can be made to feel vulnerable and unable to function without the support of the aggressor. They therefore experience trepidation around any prospect of being alone, often the reason why some people are unable to leave abusive relationships. There is an old proverb that if you are told something often enough, you begin to believe it. As a consequence of this, you can sometimes see evidence of a self-fulfilling prophecy, where the individual begins to act and live up to their label. In this instance one who is inferior, weak and unable to stand up for themselves, but it is important to recognise the use of the word 'act' here. This is not a true reflection of the individual, more a persona. It is interesting just how many clients I have worked with who after the breakdown of a relationship and several sessions of therapy, will disclose how they cannot believe they 'became that person' and 'allowed themselves' to remain in that position for such a long time. It's worth noting however, that this is not an uncommon method for an abuser to use, and is sometimes done so diplomatically the victim has very little insight into what is happening until much further down the line. I have worked with so many clients who have made these discoveries only in therapy, and some years later too. It is vital we remember this is a reflection on the abuser, not the victim.

How many have been in a relationship where we have felt criticised or where our opinions have been undermined, consequently making us feel unworthy? I would imagine many could raise their hands and say they have experienced this at some stage of their lives, within a relationship.

However at what point does this move away from a bad mood, a clash on a subject or even a frustration from a partner and become something more sinister? This is where we encounter a grey area and perhaps the very reason why the statistics we have on abuse may not be an accurate reflection of the scale of the issue. So when does it become abuse?

My clients will have often heard me refer to the concept of intent versus interpretation. I usually explore this in detail in couple therapy specifically, to try and encourage empathy and help clients to understand how their behaviour may be impacting their partner, regardless of what the intent is. So for example whilst mocking your partner's lack of culinary skills may be intended as light hearted fun, it's important to consider how that is being interpreted and consequently, the feelings this may be inducing in your partner. So when we explore the transformation of 'gentle mocking' into something more resembling of emotional abuse, I wonder whether it is when we are aware of the impact our words and behaviours have, yet we continue to exhibit them? Abuse in most cases is about power, it's about being able to have that control over people. It can also be about punishment or controlling a situation. I was saddened to recently read a post on social media which involved an individual openly stating they had lured their ex-partner to the house under the pretence of seeing his son, but would call the police to report a physical assault the moment he arrived. This had drawn a lot of ire from both men and women responding to the post, but presented a thought provoking question, relating to the perceptions of society and the authorities as to the general pattern of domestic abuse. What I mean by this, is do we still exist in a time where the response to a report of domestic abuse is not determined by the situation, but by the gender of the complainant? What is happening in wider society for this individual to have the notion that falsely reporting domestic abuse is the easiest way to exact revenge on her ex-partner, to impact him both emotionally and psychologically? Whilst this may seem like an extreme form of emotional abuse, sadly it will not be an isolated incident and highlights a serious challenge we face which detracts from those who are genuinely subjected to abuse.

There are many facets to emotional abuse, and what I would like to do now is explore a few with you. Sometimes emotional abuse can be concealed which means it is difficult to recognise and easy to misconstrue as something else. Feeling like you are in a loving relationship, can make it all the more difficult to accept that your partner may be undertaking deceitful and deliberately spiteful behaviour to try and hurt or undermine you.

However there are some common practices which abusers like to undertake, and quite often they can be mistaken for other things.

"I'm getting the silent treatment again and I've been kicked out into the spare room."

For anybody who is in a long term relationship or married, this will probably resonate with you. Of course it is not wholly uncommon for couples to argue resulting in a period of not communicating with an accompanying lack of affection. However this can also be used as a form of psychological abuse. It is a way of holding power and control over a partner to try and install certain negative emotions within them. It can be used to elicit a specific response to manipulate a situation and a person. Perhaps the key factors to consider here are the frequency this happens, whether it is one sided, and what is happening in the relationship at the time. Sometimes if you take a step back, you will be able to see a pattern within the onset of this behaviour and identify whether it is simply an argument which has resulted in mutual hurt or frustration, or whether it is something more serious and prolonged.

Relationships breaking down can be difficult at the best of times, but when children are involved it adds further complexity to the situation. Sometimes emotional abuse is not always contained within a relationship. I have worked with several fathers who have a very strained relationship with their ex-partner and have been finding building a relationship with their children increasingly difficult as a result of the way they have been portrayed. Saying disparaging things about a parent to a child with the sole intention of manipulating a situation to your advantage is a form of emotional abuse. Sometimes people may dismiss this as one parent expressing anger or not agreeing with something the other parent may have done, but those conversations should take place between the 2 adults and not between a parent and child. This can be taken a step further where one parent will say negative things about the other with the knowledge this will undoubtedly have an impact on the children. When the children consequently react in a negative manner, they then present themselves as the one to comfort and sooth the child, to make things better. With the men I have worked with, this has presented two outcomes. Firstly it has created a barrier between the father and his children. Secondly it has solidified the relationship a mother has with her children as the father is conveyed as the problem, and the mother as the solution. This has the capacity to alienate a father from his children and put a considerable strain on the relationship. I have seen the effects of this in the therapy room, and it is perhaps one of the most damaging forms of abuse I have ever worked with as it can severely impact a father's long term relationship with his children.

Accompanying this quite often is a lack of trust and a reluctance to enter into a committed relationship again in the future through fear of being subjected to the same emotional trauma. Some will even avoid having children with future partners due to the possibility of the situation arising again, an issue which can ultimately lead to the breakdown of a relationship.

Of course we should note that this form of abuse does also happen within a relationship and can be a way of gaining control and punishing an individual. Within a household it can also alienate an individual whilst conveying a very dangerous message to the children. Children in their own right, within an abusive household also become victims and there is the risk that they will sympathise with the victim, but identify with the perpetrator. Albert Bandura in 1977 developed the social learning theory, which proposes that children are influenced and will subsequently learn behaviours based on observation[34]. So effectively, behaviour observed is behaviour absorbed. However there have been challenges to this theory and it is important to recognise that not all children in abusive households will go on to be abusers. We should keep in mind however that certain environmental and social factors could well increase the likelihood of a child's behaviour being modified in accordance with what they are witnessing on a regular basis. The impact of being in an abusive household on children is something we cannot ignore or underestimate.

If a young girl witnesses repeated abuse on her mother, by her father she may normalise this, which could leave her vulnerable in future relationships. However this could also influence her in a very different way, with her vowing to never allowing a man to treat *her* in that way, risking her becoming a perpetrator rather than a victim. If she witnesses her father being abused, she may identify with her mother again normalising this behaviour (increasing the risk of her becoming an aggressor herself), or sympathise with her father, which could in turn again leave her vulnerable. Boys exposed to an abusive environment will be faced with the same permutations, highlighting the fact that abusive behaviour can often have more victims than we realise, and it is the abuse, not the gender which is the decisive factor.

"It's just a bit of banter, she doesn't mean any harm by it".

One of the challenges we have had is that previously certain patterns of behaviour which would constitute psychological or emotional abuse have not been recognised as such, and have therefore been overlooked. An example of this is perhaps something many may have been subjected to at some stage in a relationship, which is being ridiculed in front of others. Naturally there will of course be times when this is simply a reciprocal and mutually accepted part of a relationship, with no deliberately harmful undertone. Each relationship sets its own boundaries of what is and is not acceptable, and only the individuals in that relationship will know whether this is something which is meant and interpreted in good spirit, or whether there is a darker and more deliberate intention. So are there any particular signs to look out for here? Ultimately, there are several things which could determine whether this contravenes the relationship boundaries. Firstly, and perhaps most importantly, this again raises the intent versus interpretation debate. Regardless of what the intention may be, if this is something which is causing discomfort to the other person and the perpetrator is aware of this and continues, then this is abuse. Whilst for various reasons there may be an attempt to pass this off as harmless fun, in this instance it is something which is causing regular emotional pain to another and therefore constitutes abusive behaviour. The perpetrator being aware of the impact and continuing the behaviour regardless, suggests the intent may have changed from harmless fun to something more intentional, further compounding the fact it has become abusive. Another important factor to consider in this equation is the frequency. Again this would link in with the boundaries and expectations set within a relationship, and would perhaps be more likely to be determined by the recipient. If you find this is something which is happening regularly then it may well provide an indication of the intent behind the behaviour. Imagine your emotional wellbeing as a sculpture. Now consider the notion that every time you are ridiculed whether in front of others or in private, a small chip is removed. Over time that sculpture will begin to erode to the extent where it will ultimately dissipate. The damage that prolonged emotional or psychological abuse can do sometimes requires more therapy and a longer journey to emotional recovery than physical abuse does. My profession has seen me work with a range of clients subjected to both physical and emotional abuse and I have found the psychological trauma experienced through emotional abuse can sometimes be more difficult for the client to work through. One of the main reasons for this, as discussed earlier, is the fact that emotional abuse is not always easy to identify in the moment. This means the realisation of what took place in the relationship, as well as its true impact, may only begin to be unpacked during the therapeutic or any other reflective process. It is also worth keeping in mind that whilst physical abuse may in some instances be an isolated incident, emotional abuse by its very definition tends to be more synonymous with something which takes place continuously over a period of time, although of course there are always exceptions. When we consider the act of ridiculing somebody in front of others, we would ordinarily think of verbal abuse taking place in a public forum such as a bar or café or even at somebody's house at a social gathering. However as the use of social media has expanded and become more prominent, we have arguably seen an increase in the prevalence of abuse. Social media can provide an easier platform for people to perpetrate such behaviour, which adds another dimension to the issue. With relative ease you can reach a wider audience making it more difficult for victims to seek respite and feel safe. My practice has seen an increase in the amount of men attending therapy and disclosing they have been subjected to ridicule and abuse by a partner on social media. Whilst there may be varying opinions on this, what is indisputable is the emotional trauma which can be left when somebody has their sexual performance, intelligence, common sense, or even their ability to be a father or partner mocked in front of family, friends, work colleagues, acquaintances or even strangers. It can be extremely damaging and also provides uncertainty around the size of the audience reached. As a result of this there is the potential for a man to become more sensitive and hyper vigilant to any signs that his partner's mood is changing; to walk on eggshells to try at all costs to avoid this behaviour; and to make overly elaborate efforts to please or placate his partner. This can be emotionally fatiguing and has the potential to lead to a continuous state of anxiety, which is where we can see symptoms of a more psychosomatic nature appear.

Stalking and excessive contact

It's always nice to feel wanted and secure in a relationship. Those nice text messages; that spontaneous visit at work; the phone call on your way home to see how your day has gone, or even just to hear the sound of your voice; the intimate display of physical affection. In moderation and with the right intent and reception they are an invaluable part of a relationship and can indeed provide that security and feeling of being loved which so many of us yearn. However they also have the capacity to take on a darker meaning and the intent can very easily switch from something endearing to something endangering. So when should we be concerned?

- If that spontaneous visit at work for affectionate reasons transforms into something more regular and becomes more about certifying your whereabouts and actions to mask an underlying insecurity.
- If those occasional text messages become vast and overwhelming with an overt change in tone.
- If the phone calls begin to increase significantly in frequency and there are consequences if you do not answer.
- When the physical affection becomes excessive and you notice a change in their behaviour if you reject this or do not reciprocate the way they would like you to do so.

The list above is by no means exhaustive. These changes in behavioural patterns ostensibly may not feel significant, but they can constitute emotional abuse and have a profoundly negative effect on our wellbeing. Again you could present a strong argument that when it comes to stalking, the perception is of a male perpetrator and female victim. There is a societal pressure when it comes to men that attention from a woman is either a positive or a harmless thing. However this merely reinforces the stereotype and dissuades men from coming forward due to a fear of not being taken seriously. In January 2018, the BBC published an article centred round stalking and posited that around 85% of all victims of stalking do not actually report the crime[35]. Within the article the male victim discussed the psychological impact this had had on him, stating he was fearful the police would not take him seriously if he reported this. He talked about the emotional scarring left behind and whilst some people had thought it was harmless and merely unrequited attention, it had left him cautious when leaving the house and constantly looking around, ultimately no longer feeling safe. This type of emotional abuse can have a lasting and damaging effect on a person and unarguably may change the way they lead their lives. It has the potential to modify the way they behave and can leave them lacking trust in, and doubting the intentions of, others. Quite simply excessive contact and stalking is abusive behaviour, but can sometimes be difficult to identify due to it masquerading as affection and desire. It is also worth noting that some people will be more vulnerable to this type of behaviour, particularly if they have their own insecurities and a real need to feel wanted or desired. This can often mean they do not see the behaviour as abusive, more a display of affection which makes them feel secure.

Gaslighting

The term gaslighting originates from the British play by Patrick Hamilton, 'Gas light', which dates back to 1938. The play focussed on a woman in an emotionally abusive relationship where her husband would manipulate situations to make her question her sanity, convincing her she was losing her mind. He would turn down the gas lights and then persuade her she was confused and noticing things which were not there when she questioned this. As we have begun to see just how harmful to an individual's emotional state of mind gaslighting can be, the term has become more commonly used within the therapeutic setting. The reason why gaslighting is deemed to be so dangerous is that it can result in a person questioning their own sanity, increasing levels of self-doubt and significantly decreasing levels of self-confidence. Like with some of the other concepts we have discussed up to this point, gaslighting can be difficult to detect, as some will pass it off as light-hearted relationship banter, or alternatively as a genuine disparity between the recollection of events. Perhaps ironically, dismissing it as just this and convincing your partner it's just a bit of fun, is further evidence of abusive behaviour.

So what exactly do we mean by gaslighting? Gaslighting presents in many ways, but to simplify, it is a form of behaviour which attempts to make a person challenge their own cognitions and ability. Usually used as a way to keep control of a situation or person, it can lead to the victim questioning their own recollection of events, and in more extreme cases, their sanity. There are 3 common methods associated with gaslighting which are **hiding**, **changing** and **control**[36]. Breaking these down, the abuser wants to *hide* things from the victim. They seek to *change* something about the victim, effectively moulding them into something which represents the abuser's fantasy. The overall aim (a pattern we see throughout with abuse) is to fully *control* the victim.

There are times when gaslighting is actually done with positive intentions. For example if a child has witnessed a traumatic event, perhaps in the household, it is not uncommon to see parents try to convince the child it never happened, or it didn't happen in the way they remember it, in an attempt to reduce the psychological impact this may have on them. However this can be counterproductive, because it could result in the child doubting themselves or their parents, which could see subsequent trust issues within relationships in later life.

Sometimes gaslighting can simply be a variation in the recollection of an event. For example...

"You were so nervous you didn't even look me in the eye the entire night on our first date"
*"That's not true, I didn't feel nervous at all, and constantly gave you eye contact, **I think you are remembering that wrong!**"*

As we have explored previously, intent, interpretation and frequency are again important here in determining whether this is reciprocal banter commonplace within the relationship, a genuine disagreement on the recollection of an event, or something with a more cynical undertone. In any situation it is important for us to have context and the above example up to the last line (emboldened), could easily be construed as a variation in opinion not giving rise to any concern. However, if this is a more regular occurrence, if it is devoid of any reciprocity, becoming extremely one sided, if there is a deliberate intention of trying to get your partner to question themselves in an attempt for you to manipulate a situation and remain in control, this is where it would be deemed to have entered the realms of gaslighting.

As with other aspects of abuse, gaslighting is still thought of as being predominantly undertaken by males, ordinarily with female victims. The very play where the term came from perhaps propagating this perception.

Having worked with several male clients who have been victims of gaslighting, I have observed first-hand the effects which can be extremely harmful and far reaching. The most common theme was being unable to raise any issues without being told they were wrong and it was all in their head. In some cases this resulted in the client coming to therapy questioning themselves and wondering whether they were in fact the problem within the relationship, that they couldn't get things right and caused the frustration in their partner. Some who had once considered themselves extroverted suddenly became introverted and withdrawn as a result. So how do you know if you are being subjected to gaslighting in a relationship? There are several things you can look out for and perhaps a range of questions you can ask yourself. One of the common occurrences is questioning your understanding of a situation. If you find that you are justifying the other person's behaviour by questioning your own levels of sensitivity, apologising a lot for things which are not your fault or even apportioning blame to yourself, then this is sometimes a sign of gaslighting, because the very nature of it is to instil this type of self-doubt into an individual to deflect from the perpetrator's behaviour. Do you also feel that you are constantly making excuses for your partner's behaviour, either to others or to yourself? This can often be seen as a way of avoiding further exploration of that niggling doubt that something is not quite right. If you are able to provide reasons for each situation and occurrence, it can mitigate against an acknowledgement of any recurring patterns. Sometimes the self-doubt reaches such heights that you have trouble making even the most fundamental decisions without first seeking approval. This can create more of a dependency on your partner, which in itself can satisfy their need for control and reliance. Gaslighting is something which isn't always seen as having an immediate impact. It can result in the gradual erosion of self-confidence and the doubting of one's self can creep in over a period of time. This in itself offers an explanation as to why it can take a while to realise its presence. One of the techniques used within gaslighting can be positive reinforcement. This means there will be occasional praise from the abuser which can then make you question whether what you may be detecting is genuine or not[37]. The very fact this leads you to again question your own judgment or perception is further evidence of gaslighting. Whether this is something which has become more common in recent years, or its rise is more attributed to increased awareness is debateable, however one thing which is agreed upon is the very real impact it can have on an individual. Not only can it create emotionally traumatic experiences, but it can also have long-term effects on future relationships and friendships, particularly in relation to trust. It is important to be aware of some of the signs of gaslighting, because like other aspects of emotional abuse, it has the potential to be subtle in its delivery. Ultimately, you are the experts in your relationship and will also know yourself better than anyone. It is not just a case of looking for changes in your partner's behaviour, but also your own as this can often be an indication that something in the relationship has changed.

Another important aspect of emotional abuse which we will explore is something which many may not recognise as abusive behaviour. The continuous **accusations of having an affair** may to some appear as a minor and harmless frustration, a sign that your partner is insecure and vulnerable. Underlying insecurity, previous abandonment and/or attachment issues can all contribute to a person becoming emotionally abusive in this manner. We have already touched upon the social learning theory and explored how we can be shaped by previous experiences. And in these cases, whilst it still constitutes emotional abuse, the abuser may be oblivious to their behaviour and certainly unaware it could be construed as abusive.

However, there is a time when the focus shifts from that person being a victim, to them being deliberately abusive to maintain control in the relationship. As well as being characterised by an underlying fear and insecurity, it can also be characterised by jealousy, a craving for attention and a way of manipulating a situation to generate a prescribed response. It can become a repetitive cycle involving accusations, apologies, justifications and subsequent affection. Interestingly it is not uncommon to see all of the above come from the abusive partner.

So it's simply a craving for attention to mask insecurity right?

No. There are many different reasons why people would display this type of behaviour and not all may be intentionally abusive. It could be they genuinely believe that an affair is taking place and want their suspicions to be confirmed, so they have an explanation. They may seek a reason for what they have been feeling and a justification for raising those suspicions. Whilst it may not be too difficult to sympathise with somebody affected so significantly by insecurity (whether from past experiences or not), there are certainly times when the intention is much more deliberate. Accusations of this nature can be emotionally damaging to the recipient, particularly if they have always placed a great emphasis on trust, loyalty and remaining faithful. When somebody is directing a great deal of anger or frustration at their partner, you can sometimes see an intentional attempt to cause hurt to that person. This can be calculated and targeted specifically at something which you know will have an impact. This abusive behaviour is very much designed to cause the most hurt in an area where it will do just that. This behaviour is perhaps more common than you think and like gaslighting, the effect can be a slow burn. Over a period of time it can result in a withdrawal from others due to fear of the accusations, which has the potential to subsequently create a reliance on your partner. This can in turn promote social isolation, which is another key characteristic of abusive behaviour.

Have you ever been in a situation where somebody has (without justification) yelled at you and accused you of being aggressive, when in fact it is they who usually show aggression? This is what's known as **projection** and something which you may have encountered unwittingly.

It is something I have worked with and also witnessed first-hand in practice with clients. Sometimes it is challenged by a partner, other times the partner is more submissive and accepts what is being said with little objection. Either way projection can be a form of domestic abuse and can make you begin to question yourself, which of course links us back to gaslighting. So what actually is projection? Well projection is where essentially you will 'project' something you dislike in yourself onto another individual. Here is an example of projection which perhaps carries less severity.

A friend, who is well known for their tardiness, decides to vocalise their discontent at you for being late on one occasion and accuses you of continuously lacking in timekeeping skills. They are taking something about themselves and projecting that onto you.

In abusive relationships, this is very much closely linked with gaslighting as over time the victim can start to experience self-doubt and wonder if indeed they are actually guilty of that which they are being accused of. More common forms of projection involve the accusation of aggression (passive or physical), the accusation of being lazy and the accusation of having an affair. Again, here are just a few examples and there are many ways in which projection can manifest itself. The important thing to remember here is that projection is often attributed to an insecurity, or a disdain for something within yourself, and therefore projecting onto others acts as a defence mechanism, a self-preservation. Whilst you could argue that it does contain an element of control and certainly does involve a form of gaslighting, this is often as much about the perpetrator and protecting themselves than it is about gaining control over another person. Recognising this is not always easy and whilst ostensibly you might feel this is relatively harmless, projection has the capacity to have a profoundly negative impact on a person. Whether I am working with couples or individuals, when I have an inkling that projection may be occurring, one of the questions I like to ask is "How much of that do you believe is on you and how much is on them?" This tends to be quite thought provoking for the client and the moment they start to apportion some of the blame elsewhere, is the moment they become aware that actually their partner may well be projecting onto them. However, sometimes it can take months of therapy to help somebody to explore, recognise and then deal with the impact of projection. I had been working with one client for almost 3 months before they realised that their spouse had been projecting, and they had been experiencing an enormous amount of self-doubt and low moods for a long period of time as a result. The work in recognising projection is not always straightforward, but there are several things to consider to determine if you are being subjected to this. Firstly consider the frequency. Whilst projection can happen in an instant, when it is symptomatic of something more malicious, you will find it will be repetitive and consistent in its tone. Naturally we will always reflect and consider whether there is a valid point in there, or whether it is something unsubstantiated. You know you better than anyone and only you will be able to tell whether there is any truth in what is being presented to you. In addition to this, consider the timing. Is there a pattern of when this type of behaviour occurs, for example after your partner has not got their own way? Finally consider their actions present and past and determine whether actually what they are accusing you of is something which you have observed repeatedly in them. Again these are only a handful of warning signs, but they will hopefully provide you with some insight into recognising projection within a relationship.

As I have alluded to at previous junctures in this chapter, one of the challenges we face when it comes to emotional abuse is having that awareness of what falls under its umbrella, and being able to recognise when this is happening to us in a relationship. One of the more subtle aspects of emotional abuse is deliberately attempting to inflict feelings of **guilt** onto your partner. As with much of domestic abuse, this is again a tool which is used to manipulate and control a person or situation. However the rationale behind it can vary and whilst sometimes it may mask insecurity, on other occasions it may be something more intentional, such as punishment for reasons only justifiable to them. Regardless of the motive, the outcome can induce emotional turbulence and even force a victim to stay in a relationship due to a fear of the consequences if they leave. A very serious example of this is something I have come across a lot, and mainly when working with males, the threat of suicide. This is when one partner will threaten to either harm themselves or end their own life if a partner leaves them. Whilst sometimes this may be out of desperation and not in any way intended to punish the other person, it is still construed as controlling behaviour. Effectively, it can be deemed you are emotionally blackmailing somebody into staying in a relationship they may no longer want to be in, due to anxieties around your wellbeing. This type of behaviour is not wholly uncommon and some of the male clients I have worked with have spent several years in a relationship they did not wish to be in due to this very reason. Any threat of suicide is extremely serious and regardless of the intent, it is important not to trivialise or dismiss it. However there are methods you can use to try and support that person without taking on any associated guilt and it is useful for you to be able to explore these. Speaking to the individual, trying to understand what is happening with them can be a good start. Sometimes relationships are unhealthy and helping somebody to see this can be a positive thing. Alternatively if you are genuinely concerned you can always speak to their family members or even service professionals if you are worried there may be a genuine and imminent danger.

Of course, sometimes the intention of the individual is more baleful and we can observe deliberate methods to inflict guilt upon us. Signs of this can involve a consistent pattern of sulking or withdrawing if they feel they are not getting their own way or the required attention. This often surfaces when one individual may be making plans or doing something without their partner. The individual can exhibit specific behaviours in an attempt to induce feelings of guilt onto their partner to manipulate the situation, and ultimately their actions. This type of behaviour is probably something many of you will have witnessed and possibly even experienced at some stage. It is easy to dismiss it as one partner being needy or dependent, but irrespective of whether this is conscious and cynical or not, due to the very nature of it having a tendency to affect another's actions and feelings, it also comes under the category of emotional and psychological abuse. You could also provide a strong argument that this type of behaviour would fall under '**control or coercion**', something which merits its own chapter due to how prominent the topic has become in the media (ultimately influencing government policy), and the extent to which its profile has now been raised.

6

Controlling or coercive behaviour

"His family don't care, he's better without them"

"He has me, he doesn't need anybody else"

"I no longer have any friends and rarely speak to my family. I feel so isolated"

Control and coercion is something which will have been taking place both in and out of relationships for many years. One of the most challenging cases I have worked with did not actually involve an intimate relationship. Instead the individual had been controlled and coerced by a friend for several years, which had impacted in a variety of ways. Not only had they developed trust issues in subsequent friendships and relationships, but they had also spent a long period of time battling with low self-esteem and confidence. Part of the reason for this was a shame they felt that they had 'allowed' themselves to be subjected to this manipulation for a prolonged period of time without questioning it. In addition to this, they raised questions about their strength of character and ability to be assertive in conveying their own thoughts, as opposed to being submissive to somebody else's. It took several months of therapy for them to reach the conclusion that this reflected more on the other person than it did on them. They realised they had not consciously allowed this to happen, but had instead been the victim of careful and subtle manipulation. The trust and self-confidence began to build over time, but there was no mistaking the impact.

So what is controlling or coercive behaviour and why is it something we appear to be hearing more of in recent years?

There had been arguments that there were gaps in the law when it came to protecting people from domestic abuse, with much of the emphasis placed on the physical aspect, potentially omitting the emotional side. In December 2015, this was to change with the introduction of the Serious Crime Act, in particular section 76 which stated...

Controlling or coercive behaviour in an intimate or family relationship

> *A person (A) commits an offence if—*
>
> *(a) A repeatedly or continuously engages in behaviour towards another person (B) that is controlling or coercive,*
>
> *(b) at the time of the behaviour, A and B are personally connected,*
>
> *(c) the behaviour has a serious effect on B, and*
>
> *(d) A knows or ought to know that the behaviour will have a serious effect on B.* [38]

So there we have a relatively superficial explanation for what constitutes controlling or coercive behaviour, but let's look into this in a little more detail. If we look at **coercion** in the literal sense we are talking about either a single act or prolonged pattern of behaviour which is designed to intimidate, humiliate or even punish another individual. It is intended to frighten the victim into doing what you would like them to do. **Controlling behaviour** whilst sharing the same manipulative aspect as coercion, differs slightly and can sometimes be more subtle. One of the key differences when we explore control is the occurrence. Whilst coercion can be an isolated incident or a repeated pattern of behaviour, control is more specifically associated with something which takes place over an extensive period of time. One of the main characteristics of controlling behaviour is isolation. Over a period control manifests itself in the form of isolating somebody from their support network, hence increasing their dependency and at the same time reducing their means for independence. Financial abuse can also be a key characteristic of control, as it's not unusual to see access to resources and finances needed for independence, restricted or even removed completely (we will explore this further in a later chapter).

One of the key themes underpinning this book, and something we have explored in previous chapters, is this notion of intent v interpretation. This is where we can encounter a grey area, and perhaps where we find an explanation surrounding why not only is abuse under-reported, but also why it is not always recognised by the victim as abusive behaviour. A key trait possessed by people who display any type of abusive behaviour is the ability to persuade. That is to persuade the victim that how they have interpreted something is not a reflection on how it was intended. Alternatively they may make attempts to convince the victim that they are overreacting or even that their recollection is inaccurate (remember gaslighting?). When it comes to controlling behaviour, the persuasion can become more intense. The abuse may masquerade as a caring or kind nature where the victim feels that the abuser is simply looking out for them and protecting them from others who may not hold their best interests at the forefront of their minds. Abusers who may be controlling and/or coercive, as with other forms of abuse, will often seek out people who they may perceive to be vulnerable. Anybody can be vulnerable, but some may have more of a predisposition to this due to other factors. An example of this may be somebody who has had a very difficult upbringing, deprived of attention and who as a result has developed attachment injury. People who place a lot of emphasis on relationships and would consider themselves to be dependent on others may also be more susceptible to entering that position of vulnerability. I have previously been asked why people would make a conscious decision to enter a relationship with somebody who is abusive. The simple answer is that in many cases they don't. Abusers ordinarily will not show themselves in the early stages of the relationship. This can allow for the victim to let their guard down and believe they are invested in something which is equal and loving. Whether somebody has been in a previously difficult relationship and ostensibly this seems a marked improvement, or whether this is their first relationship and they have nothing to compare it to, few, if any, would make a conscious decision to enter into an abusive relationship. This is an extremely important point to raise as it compounds the fact that abuse is owned by the perpetrators and not the victims. Any move by the abuser to victim blame or even gaslight in an attempt to conceal their abusive behaviour is further evidence of them exercising control over the victim. Young people can be particularly susceptible especially when it comes to older partners (something you will see in one of the case studies at the end of this book). I spoke with somebody from the LGBT+ community who told me about their first experience with an older man when he had just come out as gay. He recalled how he was perhaps seen as vulnerable and taken advantage of physically, and the impact this had had on him. Whilst we can explore the reasons behind why abuse may take place in the first place, finding explanation does not find justification.

If we reflect back to the serious crimes act and look at sub-section 'D' in section 76, we find interesting terminology which gives further consideration to **intent**...

'A knows or ought to know that the behaviour will have a serious effect on B'

There is a clear reference here to intent when it comes to control or coercion, and this is a significant indicator that this type of behaviour can be premeditated and calculated and is by no means a reflection on the victim or anything they may have done wrong. It further substantiates that relationships may not just end up taking this route naturally, more they are carefully guided to this stage by somebody who is looking to exert coercion and/or control over another. There is a strong possibility that the abuser has either been exposed to this type of behaviour previously (potentially witnessed it within the home environment whilst growing up), or it may well mask insecurity. There is a certain parody in understanding that people who exercise control and manipulation, who exhibit what can only be described as cruel behaviour towards another, may in fact be extremely insecure and have a phobia of being alone. This is perhaps more evident when it comes to controlling behaviour where we often see an attempt to isolate an individual, reducing their chances of spending time away from, or even leaving their partner. In more severe cases where there has been prolonged and careful manipulation, the perpetrator can assume control causing complete dependence and reliance, slowly removing the opportunities for the victim to move away from the relationship and find independence.

As we have already determined, one of the key characteristics of an abuser is the ability to convince you that any suspicion you have is unjustified. Sometimes we may question ourselves wondering whether what we are thinking or feeling is an overreaction or hypersensitivity, or whether it is indeed the sign of being in a controlling or coercive relationship. If you are feeling this way, there may well be a reason for it. Even if ultimately you come to the conclusion that there is no intended malice, you are still right to raise it as clearly it is something which is affecting you. You may then consider a range of questions to come to the conclusion of whether you are being subjected to controlling or coercive behaviour:

- Is this out of character?
- Has this happened before?
- Did you feel comfortable raising your concerns and if so what was the response?
- If you didn't feel comfortable having this conversation, why do you think that might be?
- Have you noticed any other signs of this type of behaviour?
- Have other people made observations previously?

Even if you come to the conclusion that you are satisfied there was no malicious intent, it is positive that you displayed vigilance and were able to go through this process. Take pride in the fact you had the self-awareness to realise something didn't feel quite right and were confident enough to address it. If you don't feel comfortable enough to address any concerns with your partner, it is perhaps worth exploring the reason why this may be the case. Could it provide an insight into the dynamics of the relationship and what is occurring?

The Serious Crimes Act (2015), in addition to considering intent, also places an emphasis on interpretation, which will hopefully give victims the courage to come forward. It provides clear guidance on what constitutes 'serious effect', highlighting that perhaps interpretation is more important than intent in this situation. This is certainly a victory for victims as it removes the ability for perpetrators to attempt to excuse their behaviour using some of the methods we have just discussed. Here's how it allows for more focus on victim interpretation:

There are two ways in which it can be proved that A's behaviour has a 'serious effect' on B:

- *If it causes B to fear, on at least two occasions, that violence will be used against them - s.76 (4)(a); or*

- *If it causes B serious alarm or distress which has a substantial adverse effect on their day-to-day activities - s.76 (4) (b).*[39]

Whilst this legislation empowers victims and certainly seeks to address the issue of domestic abuse, we must be mindful of the fact that there are various reasons why people do not disclose or report abusive behaviour. When we look at controlling or coercive behaviour, whilst people on the periphery, may have a suspicion of what is taking place, it is not as easy for us to identify when we are emotionally invested within a relationship. Remember that many relationships do not begin in this way, more they evolve over time, with the subtlety masking the underlying intent. Quite often by the time we become aware of this, the situation may have already escalated. What may begin as your partner simply requesting you spend more time together with just the two of you, may evolve into them making comments about clothes you are wearing, places you are going, people you are seeing, and may ultimately escalate into isolating you from your friends and family. Whilst this can be done assertively, it is not always the case that we adhere through fear. Both control and coercion can also be propagated through guilt. I once worked with a client who had been in a long term relationship, afraid to end it because his partner had said she would kill herself if he were to leave. This had left him feeling trapped and suffering from low moods, unable to see a future which did not have her in it. He felt responsible for his partner and saw her as vulnerable, a victim in this situation. It was only when exploring his relationship through extensive therapy, he was able to identify a pattern of behaviour which had been evident throughout, ultimately concluding his partner had been controlling and it was in fact he who had been the victim.

One of the difficulties we can face when it comes to recognising some of the signs of controlling behaviour is having to differentiate between somebody caring and taking an interest in our well-being, and somebody serving their own agenda. There are many signs of controlling or coercive behaviour. Let's take a look at some of the less subtle ones in more detail:

For somebody who wishes to have complete control over another person, the biggest barrier they face is other people, whether that is friends, family or even work colleagues of their partner. Having other influences detracts from their control, so one of the more common signs is **isolating you from other people**. A more diplomatic method of achieving this is your partner convincing you that the other people in your life are not good for you and it is only they who you can truly rely on. Alternatively they may contact people directly and make threats, or simply behave in a way which will effectively prevent or dissuade people from contacting you. Once you have been isolated from others, you may see an attempt to diminish your self-confidence and self-esteem through continuous insults. As your self-worth declines to a significantly low level, you suddenly become reliant on your partner, believing not only are you not good enough to function independently, but also that that nobody else will want you. Another sign you may be in a controlling relationship is having your **time monitored**. This could be anything from your commute to and from work, to even being in the toilet. With the latter, not only can time be monitored, but any means by which you are able to communicate with others (such as mobile phones), may be removed from your possession. Taking longer than normal in these situations can lead to aroused suspicions and subsequent confrontation. With the associated unpleasantness of this, you will ordinarily find the victim will relent and adhere to the abuser's demands. Like other forms of controlling behaviour, there may be an insecurity which underpins monitoring somebody's time, but it can also be used as a form of punishment. If you find that time spent on your own is monitored, or even restricted, it could be a sign that your partner is undertaking abuse in the form of control. **Depriving you of basic needs and necessities** such as food, drink or appropriate warmth may also signify the presence of controlling or coercive behaviour. When we are feeling like we may have little decision making power in a relationship, one of the things we are able to control ordinarily is our food intake. Depriving somebody of basic needs is a targeted, degrading and perhaps one of the more serious forms of exercising domination over another. The abuse comes full circle when your partner may inflict severe physical or psychological trauma onto you and then **deny you access to any support services.** This is perhaps more evident in physical abuse cases when medical attention may be denied, mainly because there is a fear that the abusive behaviour may be exposed. However when it comes to male victims there is an argument that any physical injury may be attributed to something other than domestic abuse, particularly if the partner is female. Controlling or coercive behaviour is on a scale, which means that it may range from monitoring your independent time, to taking control over things such as where you can go, who you see and what you can wear. Again this could be done persuasively, or much more overtly, but the overall intention remains the same, that aspects of your life which are associated with choice and independence are being removed, with somebody else taking that control. With this particular aspect of control you quite often see an attempt at justification and sometimes you may feel they are just 'protective' or 'caring' or 'looking out for you'. In these situations it can be useful to ask yourself what happens if you acknowledge their opinion, but decide to go against it. Does it escalate into an argument resulting in you eventually relenting to pacify your partner? Is it met with silence or passive aggression? Are there other subsequent consequences? As an isolated incident we may reach a different conclusion, however if this is something which is recurrent, it may well point to control or coercion. We have already discussed how controlling behaviour can present itself in the form of emotional pressure (such as threatening self-harm or suicide), however it can also be done much more forcefully. Control or coercion can include elements of both physical and emotional abuse and can vary from subtle and gradual changes, to more sudden and explosive violence. Irrespective of the method it can be extremely damaging to individuals and can leave people feeling isolated, anxious and lacking any confidence in their own independence. It has the capacity to leave people seeking constant reassurance and validation during the rebuilding process. The emotional scarring can also manifest itself in the form of having trust and attachment issues. When it comes to attachment this is also not clear cut and could present in one of two ways. In some instances there is a reluctance to allow yourself to become emotionally attached to somebody due to a fear of experiencing the same controlling or coercive behaviour you had done previously. I have worked with several couples where this has been presented in therapy by one of the individuals and is having a profoundly negative impact on the relationship. Learning to develop that trust and allowing your partner to see your vulnerability can take time, but is possible. Almost diametrically opposed to this, are people who really struggle adjusting to being independent and self-reliant, who will ultimately seek out an attachment figure to take care of, and make decisions for them. Neither of these scenarios are right or wrong, they are just consequences of being in a controlling or coercive relationship for a period of time. However it is imperative we acknowledge that many people who have been subjected to this form of abuse will go through the process of acknowledging something is not right, proactively seeking a way out, and move on to ultimately flourish in future, non-abusive relationships, with increased levels of confidence and trust.

7

∽

Sexual abuse

"It's just a little rough play, he can handle it"

"I'm not on the pill, but he doesn't need to know that"

"My partner says men always want sex and I should be grateful"

There is no disputing that all forms of domestic abuse can have a devastating effect on the victim, but when it comes to sexual abuse, we are arguably entering a different realm, and this subject area in particular, can be highly emotive and not without contention. There have been controversies within this area with the recognition of rape within marriage (in the UK) only coming into force after a landmark court ruling in 1991[40], with it subsequently being entrenched in the Sexual Offences Act 2003. A woman giving up her right to effectively have control over her own body upon entering into marriage is unthinkable in a contemporary westernised society.

However, the controversy within this area extends into the way rape is viewed between genders. A woman cannot be charged with marital rape due to the very nature of the definition, that only non-consensual penile penetration would constitute such an offence. Whilst women can be charged with sexual coercion, causing a person to engage in sexual activity without consent and sexual assault, there are questions around the punishment which can be handed down in comparison to rape. There is also an argument surrounding the severity of which society and the legal system views rape comparatively to these crimes. Historically male victims were seen as victims of buggery and perpetrators of this act were handed lesser sentences than those found guilty of rape.

One of the common themes explored throughout this book is the notion that society in general does not like to think of men as victims. Men have all too often been thought of as strong, resilient and perhaps less likely to show emotion. This is a fallacy, and one we must address within our society if we are to obtain any balance in the way we view male and female victims. There are many factors which can contribute to an individual having strength and resilience, and whilst peers, environmental factors, family background and past experiences may make that list, gender certainly does not. I have worked with couples in some hostile situations where there has been fear, vulnerability and an inferiority complex displayed by the man, and strength, dominance and control by the woman. When we gender type, we allow ourselves to generate preconceived ideas, and these preconceptions can taint the way we view a situation. This can leave us dangerously close to overlooking victims, and by overlooking them, we are also failing them.

When it comes to sexual abuse there are several areas we are going to cover, but we will begin by elaborating on the crime of rape, introduced briefly on the previous page.

'Men cannot be raped by women'

As already mentioned, men cannot be raped by women, in any circumstance, legally in UK. The Sexual Offences Act 2003, Section 1 states the act of rape takes place if:

(a) he intentionally penetrates the vagina, anus or mouth of another person (B) with his penis,

(b) B does not consent to the penetration, and

(c) A does not reasonably believe that B consents.

The wording within the Act is very much focused on male perpetrators (note the use of the pronouns he and his), with the clear message that rape is only such if there is penile penetration.

It's worth noting that in 2020 there was a petition to change the legal definition which would allow for a woman to be charged with rape, however this failed to garner 25,000 signatures. I have no intention of debating the legal definitions within this book, it detracts from the purpose, however it's difficult to overlook the potential correlation between the legalities around sexual abuse, and societal perceptions.

Whilst any form of rape is a heinous act and can induce unthinkable trauma for the victim, we will focus on this specifically as a form of sexual abuse within a relationship. Having just defined rape, which evidently focuses on male penetration with a nonconsenting female victim, it is pertinent we also highlight rape within a same sex relationship. It is worth noting that the long-term effects of male on male rape within a relationship have had minimal research, which means its true impact is relatively unknown, leaving us only able to imagine the destruction it leaves in its wake. Although much of the basis of this book is within a heteronormative context (although we will explore abuse within the LGBT+ community at a later juncture), it appears to me as a therapist (and perhaps being a man and a male therapist are indistinguishable from my perspective), that society places less emphasis on the victim of rape or sexual assault if he is a man. So just to add a little clarity here, a male can be a victim of rape, but a female cannot be a perpetrator.

Sexual assault by penetration

The impact of a man being raped or sexually assaulted by penetration can vary and this can be attributed to several factors including the act itself, the circumstances, and of course the individual. A common misconception (and one we have addressed in previous chapters when discussing other forms of domestic abuse) is that male victims are in some way less traumatised by sexual assault than their female counterparts. This is a dangerous assumption to make, and also one which is extremely difficult to substantiate due to the fact we are dealing with something which is non-tangible and arguably unquantifiable. Whether the perpetrator is male or female, sexual assault by penetration is an extremely traumatic event and one which can have significant and prolonged effects regardless of the gender of the victim. The act is often about power and control, which in turn leaves a victim powerless and vulnerable. Whilst ever we have gender based generalisations, we run the risk of failing victims through societal assumptions. So here's an indicative example of how this may work. Due to these misconceptions, men may be wary of the reaction they may get from reporting sexual assault or rape, which means reports decrease. If the reports decline, we do not get an accurate picture of the problem and therefore available help within this area may diminish as the statistics are telling us this is not a problem which necessitates resources being dedicated to it. This can lead to some victims being more reluctant to report being sexually assaulted as they fear a lack of adequate support upon disclosure. When it comes to male on male rape, sadly I have heard people question the validity of the impact due to the individual being sexually active with other men. Essentially, if they are already engaging in said sexual activity, why should this have an adverse effect on them? A question which could be construed as homophobic, archaic and ignorant should be met with a very simplistic response. Would we ask the same question of, and apply the same logic to, a female victim who is raped having already been sexually active with other men? It is not merely the traumatic act which leaves emotional scarring, it's what it represents. It represents not being in control; it represents feeling powerless and vulnerable; it represents having no say over what happens to your own body; it represents feeling helpless; it represents somebody being able to take something against your will. We should also perhaps consider what this act means within a relationship. These apply to any rape victim, regardless of gender.

When we have sex it tends to be for one of 2 main reasons. The first being to satisfy our sexual drive, to obtain that instant gratification. Secondly, people have sex for the intimacy. It is a way of expressing our feelings for another, a way to feel close to them. Some people feel there is no better way of displaying your love for somebody, and nothing more intimate than giving your body to your partner or spouse. Of course there are other reasons as to why people have sex, which have positive connotations (trying to conceive for example), but these are arguably the main 2. However there is very much a darker side of sex and there are more sinister reasons why people partake in the act, which have little to do with the act itself. Exerting control and power over an individual is one of these and this rationale is common in sexual assault or rape. Whilst some forms of domestic abuse are a little more subtle, rape and sexual assault can be much easier to detect. Whilst you may not be aware you are the victim of gaslighting for example, saying no to sex and being forced to do it anyway is more apparent. However, like other forms of domestic abuse, it can be difficult to accept that somebody you are ostensibly in a loving relationship with could do such a thing to you. For this reason, among others, again we are faced with questions of whether or not we have an accurate picture of the true scale of male rape/sexual assault within an intimate partner relationship. Whether this is reported, whether this is an isolated incident or part of something more prolonged and calculating, the psychological impact of penetrative sexual assault or rape is extremely profound, the effects of which can be felt for many years. However when it comes to male victims, there can often be a physical response during the act which can leave them feeling even more ashamed and violated.

Men who are raped or sexually assaulted by penetration often have an unconscious physiological response which can manifest itself in the form of an erection and even ejaculation. This response is frequently used by perpetrators in an attempt to convince their victims that they were willing, or to simply try to justify their actions. Interestingly a perpetrator can also use this to convince themselves that what they did wasn't non-consensual because the victim became aroused, which must signify enjoyment. Additionally, it's not uncommon to see the victim also using this same rationale to convince themselves that they were a willing and equal participant in the sexual act. When there is a female aggressor involved in penetrating a male, any physiological response from the male can be used as an attempt to bring their sexuality into question. Effectively in this scenario there is an attempt to convince the male victim he must be gay as he became sexually aroused from being penetrated anally. This can amplify the impact as it sees the introduction of psychological abuse in conjunction with the sexual abuse with the victim being manipulated into challenging their thoughts around their own sexuality.

One thing all victims of rape and sexual assault by penetration have in common, is the act says nothing about the victim and everything about the perpetrator. Very rarely is it about sexual gratification, sex is a mere vehicle by which the assault is carried out. In life sometimes things can seem out of our control and this can be difficult to accept, but one thing which we imagine we will always have control over is our bodies. Sexual assault and rape take this away.

Coercion

Until recently, not only was it unpopular for researchers to look into male victims of sexual coercion, but some had received death threats for doing just that (Holzworth-Munroe 2005). As a result it has perhaps become evident that this is a topic which has received little focus, however its exploration plays a key role in better understanding and raising the profile of male domestic sexual abuse. Fiebert & Tucci (1998) conducted research into sexual coercion involving male victims and found 70% of the 182 participants reported having been a victim of some form of sexual coercion over the previous 5 years[41]. We have discussed coercion (along with control), in the previous chapter, but what do we mean when we talk about sexual coercion?

In simple terms sexual coercion refers to using aggressive or heavy pressure to elicit sex or sexual contact against a person's will. The key difference between this and rape or sexual assault is consent. Whilst an individual may ultimately relent and give consent, with sexual coercion it is more likely down to the excessive pressure than the desire to actually participate.

When does it stop becoming 'gentle' persuasion and become

coercion though? Perhaps a key indicator here is the frequency and vehemence of refusal. If an individual refuses to accept no for an answer and continues until they have effectively eroded the resistance and 'beaten' their partner into submission, then it escalates into something much deeper than persistence and persuasion. Coercion is something which can be difficult to measure for society, but easy to identify for the potential victim. If you have refused to participate in sexual intercourse or a sexual act and find ultimately you relent due to the overwhelming pressure put on you by your partner, this is sexual coercion; If you say yes to a sexual act for any other reason than the fact you would like to engage in it, this is sexual coercion; If you participate in a sexual act to alleviate the pressure being put on you, this constitutes sexual coercion. Guilt tripping is another method which can be used by abusers within this area. This is effectively trying to guilt a partner into complying with demands for sex or sexual contact. How exactly is this done? This can be done in several ways, whether it is verbally or by use of body language.

Perhaps they make comments about the situation with a sarcastic undertone; perhaps they question your love for them because of your refusal to participate; perhaps they use body language to show their discontent, although they don't overtly communicate this; perhaps they remind you of all the things they have done for you and question what it means that you won't comply with their request. Again the difficulty with guilt tripping as a form of coercive behaviour is understanding when the lines are crossed, the boundaries contravened. There will be many people whom have been subjected to this form of coercion, whom will feel it is either just part of the relationship or just part of the individual. If it is not recognised or acknowledged, it is much less likely to be reported. If it is not reported then it is not recorded and if it is not recorded, it does not become part of wider statistics, hence leaving us with an inaccurate picture of whether this is something which is rare or more ubiquitous.

As with many of the statistics around male domestic abuse, I question whether the figures we have are an accurate depiction of the true extent of sexual coercion involving male victims. Primarily, the reason we question statistics circles round the reporting. There are reasons why male and female victims alike do not report domestic abuse, some of which we have already discussed. However, there is another complexity added to the equation when it comes to men reporting being the victims of sexual coercion, and that is society's expectations and preconceived ideas of men and sexual gratification. In a nutshell there is a misconception that men are always available and constantly seeking out sexual fulfilment. Put simply, the perception is that men will never refuse sex and if they are engaged in sexual activity, not only is it by choice, but also quite possibly it is they who initiated it. This perception can dissuade men who may be victims of sexual coercion from reporting it through a fear of not being believed.

Punishment

The use of sexual activity as a reward or punishment is not only controversial but difficult to identify in isolation. You see in the context of a healthy relationship whilst sex can be used as a reward (perhaps a response for receiving a nice gift, gesture etc.), punishment can also have a mutually agreeable presence (sadism and masochism for example). But the key word here is agreeable and even that would need to be devoid of any coercion. Punishment in this context can enhance the sexual experience, and its presence in situations involving 2 consenting adults in itself holds no negative connotation (assuming of course no serious injuries are incurred). Sadly, however punishment in the realms of sex is not always mutually consenting and very few people are aware that as well as deliberately hurting somebody during sex to punish them, deliberately withholding sex with the sole intent of punishment is also considered to be sexually abusive behaviour. Now we need to be very clear here that this is specifically focused on intent and by no way challenges an individual's right to refuse sex. Of course simply not wishing to have sex is our very right and in no way signals abusive behaviour, but it is not the decision we are focusing on here, it is the intent behind that decision. If the sole reason of withholding sex or refusing sexual contact is to punish another individual, to deliberately harm them psychologically, that is when there are arguments we have moved into something more abusive. When the intent is to hurt somebody, to prove a point, to manipulate them in any way, to exert dominance or even to taunt them, we are displaying sexually abusive behaviour with undertones of control. We are using sex as a method of punishment and sexual activity as a form of punishment is in the intent of the perpetrator and usually in conjunction with other behaviours to enforce and maintain control. Now at this point having already explored some of the effects of other forms of abuse, (both physical and psychological), you may be thinking that not having sex in a relationship is not wholly comparable to being subjected to other behaviours like physical assault, rape, isolation, money restrictions etc. Whilst it is not appropriate or wholly relevant to rank the different forms of abuse for comparative purposes, I would like to delve a little deeper into the psychological impact deliberately withholding sex can have on an individual. Of course sex is associated with gratification and pleasure, but as we have already identified, it is also associated with love, with intimacy and with a feeling of being desired or wanted. Sex can make us feel attractive and increase our self-esteem as a result. Now in any non-platonic relationship ordinarily, there will be an expectation of sex. It is that physical aspect of a relationship, that attraction, which elevates it above a friendship. So when we are in a loving relationship and for no apparent reason the sex suddenly ceases, the first thing we do is ask the question why? Now from here we see 2 possible permutations. Firstly, we are made overtly aware that the reason for the cessation of sex is because our partner is proving a point, and once we comply this will change. Alternatively we are not aware of the reasoning behind the sudden change, which can lead to us questioning not only the relationship, but ourselves. We may question if we are still desirable or attractive, which in turn can have a detrimental impact on our self-esteem and confidence. It may also affect our ability to forge new relationships in the future. Both of these scenarios have the potential to lead to a more negative perception of sex, associating it with either control or rejection as opposed to closeness and gratification. Using sex as a punishment does not merely exist in the form of withholding it. Inflicting rough sexual acts on a partner or even pressuring them into sexual acts they may not wish to partake in, with the intent to punish that person would also fall under the category of sexual abuse. There are a variety of sexually abusive behaviours which can be undertaken as a form of punishment. These may include using sexually degrading language or even forcing your partner to watch pornography against their wishes. Like others in this book, this list is not exhaustive and in theory any behaviour or act which sees sex used deliberately with the intent to punish, whether this is physically or psychologically, may be construed as sexual abuse.

Embarrassment

How would you feel if your sexual performance was regularly mocked? Now imagine how would it feel for you if this was done so in front of others and not in the confines of a private setting? Sadly, it is not wholly uncommon for sexual activities to be used as a source of embarrassment. Phrases such as *"he can't make me cum"*, or *"he must be gay as he can't get it up"* are the types of derogatory slurs of a sexual nature that men in a sexually abusive relationship may be subjected to. Whilst some find this easy to dismiss, again the psychological impact can be significant, not only in that relationship, but in any future ones also. Developing a complex about sexual performance may result in some men shying away from future relationships or at least the sexual aspect of it, which of course has the potential to cause problems. Again there is a disparity between the way these slurs are perceived when aimed at men, and how they are perceived when aimed at women. There is an argument that when men are the recipients of such comments they are labelled as 'over sensitive'. The expectation remains that men should not be affected by comments like these, but in truth whether it is degrading or derogatory remarks or even having sexual performance ridiculed in front of others, it's not overly sensitive to have an emotive reaction to this, and certainly not unusual for this to present further challenges down the line.

In the therapeutic setting it is commonplace to work with couples presenting with issues such as a lack of desire, in both men and women. Mainly, clients who are both generally not content with their sexual activities and would like it to improve, regardless of who is ostensibly presenting with that lack of desire. However I must admit the number of couples I have worked with where the female has shown despondency at the lack of intimacy from her male partner has vastly exceeded the amount of couples I have worked with where the opposite has been presented. When I sit back and consider why this may be, I do wonder whether societal norms dictate that whilst it may be acceptable for females to attend therapy with their male partner due to him not being willing or able to have sex, it is perhaps less acceptable to see a man bring his female partner to therapy with the same complaint.

Sometimes however the lack of sex, attributed to the male, may not necessarily be through choice. Whilst conditions such as Erectile Dysfunction (ED) and Premature Ejaculation can lead to psychological trauma and a reticence to participate in sexual activity, they can also be used for ridicule and become an extension of sexual abuse. They are an obvious target, taking something which is a physical problem and making the affected individual believe this is somehow their fault, that they are inadequate. Quite naturally the feelings of inadequacy can impact self-esteem significantly. As with the previous aspects of sexual abuse, the focus is on the intent, although any suggestion that ridiculing a physical condition which is sensitive in nature is anything other than a deliberate attempt at embarrassing or belittling somebody, may be met with cynicism.

Blackmail

Most of us will know what blackmail is, and hopefully very few of us will have ever been subjected to it in any scenario. But what happens when blackmail is occurring in an intimate relationship, how does it manifest and what is its link to sexual abuse?

Blackmail in terms of sexual abuse typically refers to the threat that something negative will happen if a partner does not comply with demands around sex or sexual activity. Sex can often be seen as a commitment to an intimate partner and the absence of this quite naturally raises questions and concerns. A way to maintain control and obtain that commitment is to blackmail a partner into having sex using fear as a weapon. This can be done in a variety of ways, one of which involves using the threat of infidelity. So for example:

> *"If you don't want to have sex, there are plenty of other guys who will have sex with me".*

This essentially corners an individual and forces them into making a choice between either relenting, or facing the prospect of their partner initiating sex with somebody else. If you have a strong attachment to your partner (many involved in abusive relationships do), this can be an extremely painful choice you are faced with. The perpetrator knows this.

Other methods of blackmail may surface if we are dependent

on our partner, whether it is financially, for housing or even an emotional dependence. We may be blackmailed into engaging in sexual activity through fear of becoming homeless or destitute, or even isolated. As in many instances, abusers can manipulate a situation to create a dependency, and vulnerability. The prospect of being isolated and vulnerable can prove too much for some, resulting in them doing anything to preserve what they have, regardless of whether it is abusive or not.

Sexual abuse comes in many forms, each with the potential to have severe ramifications for the victim. One of the more serious aspects of this which we are yet to address, is women who deliberately mislead men in relation to contraception. So essentially here we are talking about women who state they are on the contraceptive pill when they are not, with the sole intention of getting pregnant. As well as being deceptive, this is arguably a form of sexual abuse which can have the most lasting and life changing effects on a man's life. I have worked with more than one male in practice who has fallen victim to this. I have also worked with women who have disclosed to having deliberately stopped taking the contraceptive pill without informing their partner, with the sole intention of getting pregnant. There are many reasons why a woman may do this whether it is getting pregnant to try to save a relationship, making it more difficult for their partner to leave, or deliberately punishing a partner who may not want children. Even if the rationale is simply wanting a child, becoming a parent is life changing and when this is not a collaborative decision, it enters the realms of deceit and deception. Sometimes it is not as clandestine as this, and in a more overt way, you may be forced or coerced into not wearing a condom, something which also constitutes sexual abuse.

Remember sexual abuse is not merely a physical act and some of the most damaging aspects of it can be more from a more emotional perspective. It is quite ambiguous in nature and relies heavily on intent, although things such as coercion are more determined by the victim, regardless of what the intent may be. Because of its ambiguity, it is difficult to measure and as with the other forms of abuse we have discussed, it relies heavily on people being aware they are being subjected to the abuse in the first place. But as with the other types of abuse we have explored, hopefully you will now have more of an insight into this area and can be more vigilant, both for yourself and for others. Recognition provides a better opportunity at acknowledgement and this is an important step on the way to feeling comfortable enough to disclose.

8

~~

Financial abuse

"I am told I am no good with money and am responsible for the financial hardship"

In 2018, Mankind Initiative (a charity specifically dedicated to supporting male abuse victims and raising the profile of male domestic abuse) reported that 17% of calls to their helpline were in relation to financial abuse. This was higher than sexual abuse (3%) and coercion or control (13%) combined[42]. Yet you could argue that sexual abuse and coercive or controlling behaviour are much more prominent within the media, perhaps culminating in a lack of awareness around other forms such as financial abuse. So what is financial abuse and how do we know if we are in a financially abusive relationship?

In many relationships there may well be one partner who keeps watch over the finances ensuring things such as the mortgage/rent and bills are paid, somebody who is cautious over monthly expenditure. After all, not all of us are financially savvy, and sometimes we welcome somebody who may be financially astute and adept at budgeting. This is a perfectly common sight in many households and within this context, may not necessarily present any problems. As with the previous forms of abuse we have explored, we again find ourselves delving into the notion of intent in order to obtain a broader understanding. This type of domestic abuse is perhaps not as recognised as others, it is not widely reported in the media and on the whole, can be difficult to detect. So how do we begin to define financial abuse? An intelligible definition is:

'any behaviour which controls, exploits or even sabotages an individual's ability to access economical resources'.[43]

One of the more common examples of financial abuse you may see involves family members and their elderly relatives. Withholding money for personal financial gain is a sad, but not uncommon occurrence within society, and because in these instances the victims are elderly and ergo also vulnerable, it can often go unnoticed. However, less widely documented are the cases of financially abusive behaviour which involve spouses or partners. Financial abuse does not only manifest itself as withholding money from a partner. It can also be present in the form of one partner manipulating or forcing another into entering into a financial agreement for an item or service. One of the challenges we face in these circumstances is it is extremely difficult for financial institutions to scrutinise any individual or joint financial agreement. To put this more simply, they lack any real power to investigate the family situation prior to document signing. Any coercion will likely remain surreptitious and once the agreement is signed, there is a legal obligation with potential consequences should this be reneged on. The effects of financial abuse can be categorised into 2 areas. The **financial effects** can be severe and may result in an individual having financial responsibility for debts they are simply unable to afford. As well as the standard of living a person may be forced into due to the financial restraints, there may also be more long term consequences which could affect a person's credit rating. This in turn could impact their ability to either obtain finance for large purchases, or more severe, a mortgage. My experience in practice has involved several clients who have been left with many thousands of pounds worth of debt, which they are likely to be paying off for many years due to financial abuse encountered in a previous relationship. Whether they have been pressured into signing for cars they don't drive, houses they no longer live in, leisure services they have never used or items they do not own, financial abuse has left them in a very precarious situation and has had a profound impact on not only their present, but potentially their future also. Again we must stress that this form of abuse, like others already covered, may not only affect a person's current relationship, but subsequent ones too. When we explore abuse and its effects, it is imperative we look beyond the current situation. Financial abuse has the potential to cause significant issues in future relationships, particularly if you are still encountering financial difficulties as a result. So, for some, the end of the relationship is not necessarily the end of the problems, and they can be faced with daily reminders of the extent of the abuse. Whilst the **psychological effects** of financial abuse are difficult to measure, it could be argued with some degree of certainty they can be just as severe. On one hand you may experience trepidation around how you are able to manage any financial commitments and the consequences if you are not in a position to do this. Accompanying this can be the emotional burden of trying to understand and rationalise how somebody who you were intimately involved with, somebody who you may have relied on for support, somebody who you may share children with, could deliberately leave you in such a financially precarious position. This in itself can be difficult to conceptualise and can quite often prove a bigger challenge than fulfilling any financial obligations you may have been left with. The realisation we may have been involved in an abusive relationship quite often presents more questions than answers, and this can be difficult to accept. What it also has the capacity to do is prompt us to formulate our own answers and create our own narrative, which may not be wholly accurate. If there have been other forms of abuse evident within the relationship, we may begin to self-blame for the situation, absolving the abuser of any fault. Remember one of the strategies abusers use is to convince the victim that they are at fault, something which can etch away at an individual's self-confidence and self-belief. If that becomes a learned behaviour, a default state of mind for any given situation, then it is understandable how you would question yourself for any far reaching consequences of the relationship. Even if we reach a stage where we acknowledge the abusive behaviour, we may still direct the anger inwardly feeling at best we were naïve and at worst, knowingly allowed this to happen. A relationship ending does not necessarily symbolise a clean break from the effects of that relationship and it's perfectly natural to take 'baggage' into future relationships. Feeling a need to control your own finances and a reluctance to commit to anything financially with another partner is a normal effect of coming out of a financially abusive relationship and it is important you are able to acknowledge this. It may not necessarily be a reflection on your partner, just further evidence to highlight the extent to which we may be influenced by past experiences. It can be difficult to trust others, especially when it comes to anything with a financial element and again this is an understandable and very natural reaction. If the financial implications are ongoing, you may be faced with a daily reminder of not just what happened, but what can happen again. The fact you are having these thoughts and exercising this caution means you are now more aware of some of the warning signs and therefore have a better chance of protecting yourself against being the victim of a similar experience.

Before we explore in greater detail some of the signs of financial abuse, it's perhaps pertinent for us to take a moment to try and understand why somebody may perpetuate this behaviour. Like the other forms of abuse we have covered, financial abuse has undertones of a need to control and some may argue if you control the finances, to a large degree you control the person. Much like emotional abuse, financial abuse also has an intention of creating a reliance on the perpetrator, or manipulating a situation for personal gain. Its focus is very much on stripping away an individual's access to resources, which would allow them to be independent. This in turn creates dependence and can decrease the options available to the victim. If they have also been isolated, it is likely they feel there are no other options, but to remain in the relationship, which means at this point the abuser has gained control. As we have already highlighted, the rationale behind this type of behaviour can vary, and whilst sometimes we can see this as punishment or retribution for a perceived wrongdoing, it is important to acknowledge that it can also mask a deep rooted attachment injury which may have originated from previous trauma (abandonment for example). Sometimes the intent may not necessarily be to punish an individual, but more to protect the perpetrator from being abandoned. This of course only provides explanation, not justification and irrespective of the intent, financial abuse can be very frightening and disempowering for the recipient. Not only can it leave people feeling wholly reliant on another person, but it can also strip them of dignity with not having any control over their own finances and having to ask for the most basic of things. As with other forms of non-physical abuse, its effects can be lasting and can impact self-esteem and self-confidence as well as a person's ability to ultimately be independent. Of course there are occasions when financial abuse may be used as a direct method of punishing you. When we feel we have been wronged, one of the things we have ability to do is to try to consider the methods we can use which will potentially cause most hurt. Making concerted efforts to strip a person of their independence, hence leaving them reliant is one such method. Financial abuse also has a very significant aspect of control to it and by stripping away a person's access to any resources which allows them to be an individual can not only cause humiliation, but also deprive them of their very basic human rights. This control is both severe and malicious, yet still there is an argument there is much less awareness in this subject area regardless of the presence of both physical and psychological effects, which can devastate an individual.

You may be forgiven for feeling that financial abuse is in the main about controlling the finances of another person and limiting/restricting entirely their access to any monies, even their own. However it runs deeper than this and can extend into restricting or limiting access to any resources for an individual (phone, car, computer for example). Sitting within this would be affecting your ability to earn money in the first instance. Whether it is sabotaging your work, by deliberately making you late, or constantly calling you to deflect your focus, or even calling your employer to disclose personal details or accusations about you; whether it is pressuring you to quit using a variety of spurious reasons, which only serve to suit their own agenda and tighten their control; whether it is dictating where and when you work, significantly limiting your opportunity for employment; or whether it is telling you that you are no good at your job and may as well quit before you are ultimately dismissed, these are all tantamount to financial abuse and highlight a strong element of control as well as a desire to diminish any individuality. Again we revisit the importance of recognising the presence of the emotional abuse within financial abuse. It has the potential to cause a person to become completely dependent on another and realising this can be extremely difficult to process. In addition to this it can also have an impact on somebody's dignity, having to seek permission for even the most basic of things which most of us will take for granted. This in turn can lead to self-doubt and a very negative perception of the self, which can in some cases take a significant amount of time to address.

Whilst we have taken a superficial look at some of the aspects of financial abuse, we should not omit the exploration of some of the warning signs which may indicate you are involved in a relationship of this nature.

Perhaps the most apparent sign of financial abuse is if one person has complete control of the household income and expenditure. Again the focus here is on control and manipulation and should not be confused with a mutual agreement within the household regarding financial matters. As we have previously ascertained, inevitably, there will be some families where one person will perhaps be more adept at budgeting and have a deeper knowledge of anything relating to finance, and this in itself does not necessarily constitute financial abuse. It enters that realm when this is not a result of a mutual agreement and is done with the sole intent of maintaining control over another, deliberately limiting or restricting that person's ability to access money or obtain resources. Additionally, you may also see one partner need to seek permission to access any money or make any purchases. Whilst this can be humiliating and degrading for the victim and has its roots set in financial abuse, there is a significant element of power and control contained within it. This moves beyond merely controlling the finances and enters into the arena of controlling the individual. If you are at a stage where you are seeking permission to access your own finances and are unable to control purchases of even the most basic of things, you may be the victim of financial abuse. It's worth considering whether you feel the relationship is balanced, as if somebody is financially abusive, you will likely see evidence of other forms of abuse which sit alongside this such as emotional/psychological, control or coercion. Control is often the one key characteristic evident in all forms of abuse, so you may be able to identify patterns of this elsewhere within your relationship. Any abuse can in some form take away individuality, whether that is through a fear of expressing yourself due to the repercussions, or being controlled (by physical or emotional means) in relation to what you can and cannot do. We have established that some abusers will try to limit or deny access to finances, but let's explore in more depth the potential implications of this. Buying clothes, food, having a mobile phone, a car and even buying presents for special occasions may be something most will take for granted, but all of these things are determined by your ability to access the relevant funds. These are things which denote independence and allow you to be able to have that degree of freedom in things you eat, places you visit, people you socialise with and in general how you are able to communicate with others. Maintaining control over the finances is sometimes done in a diplomatic manner, which means it is not always easy to detect. As a result of this, there will be an inevitable disparity between the amount of financial abuse reported and the actual instances. However what exercises less diplomacy is when you are directly denied access to things ike a car, mobile phone or even your own bank account. This is arguably the more severe end of financial abuse and can be undertaken for personal financial gain, or to develop complete control over another. Even in the situations where there may be a degree of autonomy when it comes to accessing your own finances, this can often become a false economy with either every expenditure scrutinised, or only being allowed to access a certain amount in the first place. This can leave individuals feeling guilty for spending even small amounts of money and may result in a reticence to do so moving forward. What people may fail to realise here is the impact such a scenario can have on somebody. It is not simply about feeling guilty for spending any money, but has deeper roots in the form of how the individual feels undertaking any act which may be of benefit to themselves. Put simply, they may be programmed emotionally to feel any act which may remotely serve their own interests is in fact selfish and therefore should not occur. There is a pattern emerging here highlighting how controlling the finances can lead to removing a person's independence. You may now also be starting to get a picture of how damaging financial abuse can be on an individual emotionally and how the effects, which may be long term, are not simply monetary ones. Revenge and punishment are words often synonymous with abusive behaviour and sadly it is not so unusual to see a partner take a measured consideration as to what may have the biggest impact, produce the most damage and cause the most anguish. Credit ratings and financial records can be extremely important to a person when it comes to things like credit cards, mortgages, store cards, effectively anything being financed as opposed to being purchased outright. Therefore default payments can have a potentially cataclysmic effect for future purchases of any significance. A partner, who deliberately defaults on payments, particularly when the account is in either your name solely or has joint responsibility, is displaying financially abusive behaviour. Again this could present itself in more than one way. Perhaps the most apparent way is simply by them ceasing the payments whether this is temporary or a permanent cancellation. Alternatively they could cause the default in a more indirect way. More passive aggressive behaviour such as not contributing to something which holds joint financial responsibility can be just as serious in its impact. When you consider things such as phone bills or the internet for example, it may be possible for the other person to cover the shortfall. However when we start looking at the potentially significant financial demands associated with other commitments such as car loans or rent/mortgages, it can make this much more problematic. With the latter, often a fear of the repercussions not just financially, but the very real threat of being faced with eviction or repossession can force us to relent and make what concessions we feel necessary. Whether it is for revenge, punishment or just to prove a point, this element of financial abuse can see one partner exercise control over another through fear, and whilst it may be a different kind of fear than that associated with physical abuse, it is fear nonetheless and can still prove extremely damaging. Ordinarily we associate abuse with action, but actually sometimes inaction can have an impact just as severe. Keep in mind one of the reasons that people do not report abuse is because they are unaware of it taking place. Much of this can be attributed to the fact there has not always been the available literature which highlights the different forms of abuse which exist along with accompanying behaviours. This has meant people may be victims of abuse without even knowing it. It is because of this very notion that there is a strong argument to suggest that the figures surrounding abusive behaviour per se only capture a very small portion of the actual abuse which takes place within society. So when a partner continuously reneges on contributing financially to anything associated with the home or the relationship, many of us may see this as frustrating, or even determine that they contribute in other ways. At worst we may acknowledge this as passive aggressive behaviour and question their reliability. However this 'inaction' would constitute financial abuse. Remember this form of abuse aims to limit or restrict a person's ability to maintain or utilise finances, and in this example the refusal to contribute in monetary terms may well place excessive financial burden on an individual which will ultimately affect their ability to maintain their money. Sometimes there may be selfish motives behind this (wishing to save the money to spend elsewhere on themselves). However, If the household is reliant on duel income, yet the utility bills and/or mortgage are in one name, withholding money can either be used as leverage to obtain something (which certainly denotes control), or alternatively to knowingly punish a partner or spouse, fully aware of the impact of this behaviour. Other forms of financial abuse may involve such things as opening store cards or other credit cards in your name and running up excessive bills, which you are potentially then liable for. Opening up catalogue accounts and spending large amounts, or even installation of media services such as TV, broadband or telephone, may also be signs of financial abuse. Even if these have been done with your prior knowledge or consent, it may still be abusive behaviour if you have been coerced. Take a step back and consider whether this was something you were wholly in agreement with or something you felt obligated to do. Is there any financial contribution from your partner, or are you liable for the whole amount? It is also worth considering whether it's something you will utilise and benefit from or something that is solely in the interest of your partner. If you are concerned you may be the victim of financial abuse, it's worth asking yourself how much control you have over your finances; what is the contribution from your partner?; how often do you talk about money and is this a reciprocal and balanced conversation or more one sided?; If you wanted to make a spontaneous purchase, would you have access to the resources to do this and would you feel comfortable doing it without seeking prior permission? Financial abuse can create a dependency in the way it exercises control over another. One of the challenges we face with this form of abuse is that we cannot question that which is unknown to us, and sometimes this abuse is unknown to us. It is possible that by the time we become aware of it, there may have been significant damage either from a financial aspect or a psychological one. However, even though financial abuse has the capability of creating a dependency, because its profile is being raised, there are now more options available for support, both financially and emotionally.

9

~

Domestic abuse within the LGBT+ community

"I understand him, I'm not abusive"

"He shouldn't have embarrassed me"

"This is just how it is in the community and what happens in relationships"

When we consider domestic abuse, it would be naïve of us to think that all female victims have male aggressors and vice versa. This mind set assumes all relationships to be of a heterosexual nature and therefore runs the risk of overlooking the LGBT+ community when it comes to studying domestic abuse. There are several explanations as to why prevalence of domestic abuse within the LGBT+ community may be relatively unknown. There is little media coverage on this topic, and literature which accurately reflects the figures may be extremely difficult to locate. Like when we look at abuse holistically, one of the main challenges we witness is a reluctance to disclose or report. However, in this instance there may be additional complexities which means speaking out may be even less common and more difficult. I recently conducted a small survey (too small to be generalisable), but was interested to see that of the LGBT+ participants who had disclosed being in an abusive relationship, many had not reported it at the time, with the main reason being they had not realised they were the victims of abusive behaviour until afterwards. This further highlights the need for more literature and more awareness.

What I would like to do in this chapter is shine the light on abuse involving those identifying as male, whether perpetrated by a partner, or targeted through family. I have worked with several transgender clients previously and hearing them recount their experiences, particularly within the family environment is both powerful and emotional. I was privileged to have been able to interview a young man who shared his experience of domestic abuse when in a previous same sex relationship. You will be able to read about this in detail in the 'case studies' section at the end of this book. The interview was extremely insightful and gave me more of an understanding into not only the forms of abuse which occur within same sex relationships, but also the rationale behind why this may be so under-reported.

What does the data tell us about domestic abuse within the LGBT+ community?

Domestic abuse research suggests that rates of under-reporting within the LGBTQ population are between 60-80% (Galop, 2020). In 2019, Safelives[44] published a datasheet highlighting that of all individuals who were accessing support for domestic abuse, only 2.5% identified as LGBT+[45].

Haringay Council published a briefing in 2017, highlighting that data shared at a Multi-Agency Risk Assessment Conference had shown that 3% of all reported domestic abuse incidents within the area in 2015/2016 had been LGBT+ cases[46]. This was 2% above the national average, which may raise the question of why only 3 lines out of the entire document were dedicated to this.

A survey conducted by the charity Stonewall capturing data from 2008-2011 found that 49% of all gay and bi men had experienced (since the age of 16) at least one instance of domestic abuse, either from a family member or partner[47]. Galop's domestic abuse report (2018) found that of those victims who had reached out to the charity (circa 626), 65% were male with 55% of these identifying as gay men. A staggering 79% of this abuse was categorised as intimate partner abuse with 87% disclosing emotional abuse and 71% stating they had been subjected to physical abuse. What is also interesting is the fact that 82% of lesbian women disclosed domestic abuse from a female perpetrator[48].

Do we have an issue with the reporting of same sex domestic abuse?

Exploring this question will take us naturally into highlighting some of the signs of same sex domestic abuse. Whilst the emphasis will be around same sex male domestic abuse, this in no means precludes relationships which may involve transgender individuals who identify as male. It is important for me to be perspicuous in the point that when I talk about male domestic abuse I am referring to anybody who identifies as male, whether this is through biological sex assigned at birth, reassigned sex or the social construction of the male gender.

To understand why same sex male domestic abuse is arguably significantly under-reported, we first need to look at the '*additional complexities*' I referred to at the beginning of this chapter. In previous chapters we have discussed some of the reasons as to why people do not always report domestic abuse, some of which have included a fear of the consequences, a concern they will not be believed, an emotional connection to the abuser and not being aware they have been the victims of an abusive relationship at the time. In May 1988 the 'Local Government Act 1988'[49] introduced section 28, arguably even more contentious now looking back retrospectively. Section 28 prohibited local councils or schools from advertising or actively promoting homosexuality. This meant that many gay people were extremely cautious of their behaviours and actions through fear of repercussions. In addition to this, teachers became reluctant to intervene in homophobic abuse within the playground, feeling they couldn't step in. The message was clear; society needed to promote 'traditional' nuclear family values, but some inferred this as a license to undertake homophobic, transphobic or biphobic abuse. Section 28 remained in law for 15 years until it was finally repealed in the latter part of 2003; however there are strong arguments that section 28 had catastrophic effects on the LGBT+ community which would be felt for years to come (some argue this is still felt today). Young gay men were leaving school confused about their feelings as they were unable to discuss their sexuality and overcome what is tantamount to a denial that 'gay people' existed. This meant young adults were seeking advice and comfort online which opened them up to other potential threats. At the end of this book you will read the story of Toby, a man subjected to emotional and physical abuse when he entered his first same sex relationship as a youth. Prior to this Toby had begun talking to, and subsequently met with somebody whom he had encountered online. His drink had been spiked and he was sexually assaulted. This was never reported. One of the things Toby discussed with me was a fear of discrimination from the police and how he would be treated. Toby felt like this was one of the reasons why more people from the LGBT+ community did not come forward and report domestic abuse.

Same sex marriage was not legalised in the UK until 2013, and whilst you could certainly put forward a convincing argument that as a society we have become more accepting, there are still those who will hold what some would describe as archaic views of what the family and a relationship should look like, particularly in cases of religious influence. For this reason, there are some who will not openly come out as gay to their family members, work colleagues or even friends. This in itself may have a significant impact on the decision to report any domestic abuse through fear of being 'outed'. Imagine having to make a decision whereby you are considering whether the domestic abuse you are being subjected to is preferable to the consequences of suddenly having your sexual orientation exposed to others. Sadly, there still exists an intolerance which is reflected around the globe with some countries imposing the death penalty for those found to be involved in a same sex relationship. 'Outing' within the realms of domestic abuse is multifaceted. As well as the fear of being outed during the reporting stage, it can also be used by the abuser as a form of control. Knowledge that a male partner may be taking measured and extensive steps to keep their sexuality private can effectively provide an opportunity for the abuser to exercise control through fear. The very threat of being outed to family, friends, work colleagues, religious communities or perhaps recreational groups can result in compliance within a relationship. This is a form of psychological abuse as well as controlling behaviour and can mean that somebody stays in a relationship they do not wish to be in through fear. In addition to this, they may also be subjected to things they are not accepting of, but comply with through that fear. The victim can suddenly feel powerless realising they may not have control over the disclosure of their sexual orientation.

There is an argument that the LGBT+ community can be seen as quite insular, which may limit the support available to the victim. If they have been marginalised within the community through the abuser, this limits the support further, and significantly. Ultimately it becomes a choice between accepting things as they are, or facing the fear of having your sexual orientation exposed, along with any repercussions of this. It is also worth noting that reporting abuse in such a close-knit community may result in being further ostracised. We have explored in detail how one of the key components within domestic abuse is isolation. That is, abusers seeking to gain control by manipulating the situation to ensure that the victim is removed from family, friends, co-workers and any social events. This can be done in several ways whether it is overtly enforcing it, removing resources (such as phones, Wi-Fi, tablets etc.), which would give them access to the aforementioned, or whether it is in a more clandestine way using the power of persuasion. When we look at the LGBT+ community, as we have highlighted already, we may be looking at a much smaller circle for potential support. Isolation in this instance may come in the form of preventing the attendance of any events or even restricting literature which would keep them abreast of things which may be happening within the community. The victim may feel shame they are experiencing this and begin to question whether this is something which is self-inflicted as opposed to the fault of the abuser, particularly if they are ostracised from, or castigated by, the community. Isolation can be more prominent if you have a couple where one male is already well established in the community with the other being in their first same sex relationship and being relatively new to it. Regardless of the rationale behind isolation, this can have catastrophic consequences. In July 2020, the BBC produced an article stating the number of people within the LGBT+ community seeking suicide prevention support had increased significantly during the lockdown period[50]. It is thought one of the main reasons for this is not feeling connected to the community, resulting in a lack of support. Whilst it is encouraging people are seeking help, sadly many have not and there has been a growing concern of the increase of suicides within the community.

Whether it is due to society's portrayal, parental attitude or even personal experience growing up, it is not uncommon to see shame experienced by some people who have been struggling with their sexuality. Remember shame is not be confused with guilt. Guilt is something which arises from behaviours or actions. So we may feel guilty about a specific behaviour (cheating on our partner for example). Guilt is something which is very much contained internally and something more often than not we put on ourselves. Shame on the other hand is more associated with the person we are. It moves away from a single act and takes on a more generic meaning about who we are as a person. When you begin to explore the concept of shame in detail you find that in many instances it is something which can be put on us by others. What I mean by this is that shame can come from a variety of places such as societal expectations, family values, religion, culture etc. So if we are made to believe that being gay is not right and that our sexuality has impacted other people in a negative way, we may feel shame about being the person we are. The consequences of this can be profound and may vary from repressing who we are and living as we feel others expect us to live, to being overcome with shame to such an extent, we are unable to deal with it.

So how does this link in with domestic abuse? It is perhaps more pertinent to look at shame in the context of why male domestic abuse within the LGBT+ community may be under-reported. We have explored how some men may feel isolated from the community or fear alienation or judgment if they speak out about abuse. We have also explored how a fear of having our sexuality disclosed to others, without us having any control over the narrative may result in a compliance or acceptance of an abusive relationship. However what we haven't yet addressed is the fact that some people may feel like they are deserving of the abuse, and that is where we are able to discover the link between shame and domestic abuse. In these instances the abuse will become associated with the gender they choose to live as or their sexuality. The shame which may be inflicted upon them by family or wider society may be enough for them to internalise and use as justification for the abuse. Ergo, they feel they are deserving of the abuse because of the fact they may be gay or transgender and if they were not, they would not be encountering it. This thought process can sometimes escalate and actually create an internalised hatred of your sexuality. This in turn, in some instances can result in inward feelings of homophobia, biphobia or transphobia.

Another key consideration is the fact that domestic abuse isn't well recognised in the LGBT+ community. Arguably part of the reason for this is due to the media portrayal of domestic abuse and the feeling that as most literature purports to heterosexual women being victims, domestic abuse in the LGBT+ community is not wholly represented. This presents a problem in itself. The aggressor may be oblivious to the fact their behaviour constitutes domestic abuse. They may instead feel either it is a natural part of a relationship, or that ultimately their behaviour is not negative. Victim blaming is one of the ways domestically abusive individuals justify to themselves (and the victim) that their actions were necessary and that the other person was responsible for this, not they. So by absolving themselves of blame and in turn accountability, they feel their behaviour is not out of the ordinary in that situation. This can allow an abuser to live without conscience because they are impervious to the fact they are domestically abusive. This of course is only one possibility and there are so many variables within abusive behaviour, we need to be very careful to not make the same assumptions surrounding the circumstances of all domestically abusive relationships. Antithetical to this would see an abuser being aware of their own behaviour, but also being aware it is not widely recognised within the LGBT+ community and using this to their advantage. So in essence we are referring to the displaying of abusive behaviours intentionally and purposefully, knowing the full impact. This can be done to try to gain or maintain control within the relationship using the holistic lack of awareness as an advantage. The lack of coverage for domestic abuse within the LGBT+ community can serve as a disadvantage to victims, but an advantage to perpetrators. Victims may already feel marginalised, and if they have been ostracised from families and friends, may be more likely to accept the abuse as part of the relationship, due to fear of being completely isolated. The challenge we have with this is that as a result, some victims within the LGBT+ community will not see themselves as victims, instead feeling that this is part of a relationship. Many within the community do not recognise domestic abuse as being present in LGBT+ relationships. This certainly runs the danger of any type of abusive behaviour being normalised, which can make addressing it more difficult. A result of this can be a lack of knowledge in how to respond if there is that recognition that abuse may be taking place in a relationship involving a friend or loved one. We have already discussed how difficult disclosure and reporting can be, so imagine adding another level to this in the form of a fear of being ostracised by an entire community. These are some of the hidden complexities I alluded to earlier in the chapter.

Examples like these perhaps provide us with a more clear insight into why some people within the LGBT+ community are more hesitant to disclose or report domestic abuse. Throughout this book I have advocated a more consolidated, non-gendered approach to tackling domestic abuse, and the LGBT+ community must be included within this. The arguments outlined within this chapter would suggest careful consideration needs to be given to ascertain how you can actively involve the community in tackling domestic abuse.

Whilst undertaking research for this chapter I came across a very powerful real life story which I wanted to share with you. It was a very short interview with a male survivor who discussed his abusive relationship with another man. He speaks about being physically assaulted, being prevented from working and having his phone taken from him. In addition to this he was isolated from others[51]. This pattern of behaviour may be sounding familiar as we conclude this chapter, but it's imperative we are able to raise awareness not only of the problem, but also of the help and support available. This individual through the support of a domestic abuse helpline was able to leave the abusive relationship and begin a new life for himself, showing that by enhancing levels of awareness around abusive behaviour whilst providing clear indication of organisations that can help, we can start to reach out to victims. There exists a slightly different proposition here when addressing domestic abuse within the LGBT+ community. That is the focus perhaps needs to be as much targeted within the community as it does external to it.

10

∽

Moving forward - What needs to change?

"*Change will not come if we wait for some other person or some other time. We are the ones we've been waiting for. We are the change that we seek*" - **Barack Obama**

"*I cannot say whether things will get better if we change; what I can say is they must change if they are to get better*" - **Georg C. Lichtenberg**

Any mention of abuse ordinarily elicits an emotive reaction and the subject area has generated much debate as to how it should be addressed. I want to specify that the purpose of this book is not to apportion blame to any specific institution; we are simply exploring reasons and seeking explanations which may be built around previous experience or perception. The intention of this book is not to criticise in any way the fantastic work many charities dedicated to tackling domestic abuse do; it is to try and link that work together to form something less fragmented and more collaborative. This book does not seek to cause a gender divide, but to tackle a gender divisive approach. I want to highlight the issue of male domestic abuse and draw attention to the challenges ensconced within it, but not at the expense of female victims or the charities that support them. We need collaboration, not division.

Domestic abuse is not simply limited to physical violence. That lack of visibility can make it harder not only for others to detect from the periphery, but also for many victims too. All too often victims don't realise they are victims and accept it as being part of the relationship. Or they simply attribute it to being part of the individual and don't recognise it as being abusive behaviour. We must distinguish here between when a victim does not recognise abuse and when they do not acknowledge it as these two terms can carry very different meanings, certainly in this context. When I make reference to recognition, I refer to being unaware that one is the victim of domestic abuse. As we have discussed, sometimes abuse can be carried out in a very covert and subtle manner. If you couple with this a partner who may be ostensibly charismatic and caring, it can make detection much more difficult. For long periods we have primarily associated domestic abuse with physical violence, and as a result of this some of the other forms have often flown under the radar, because we are programmed to look for tangible evidence. Historically, acts such as belittling, deliberately embarrassing, body shaming, keeping complete control over the finances, turning children against a parent and even deliberately withholding sex as a punishment, have not been recognised as being abusive behaviour. Some may be seen as unkind, others perhaps not even acknowledged at all. To promote awareness, we first have to have society wide acknowledgement of what constitutes domestic abuse and what is and is not acceptable within a relationship. Once we have that, and only then, can we begin to raise awareness to reach out to people who may be vulnerable or in a domestically abusive relationship. Recognition is the first step and it highlights to the victims that what they may be experiencing is not conducive to a loving relationship and does not have to be accepted. Ultimately one of the key aims of this book is to provide a more in depth understanding of what an abusive relationship looks like. Naturally some of the content will resonate with people and for those whom it does; hopefully it provides an opportunity for you to re-evaluate your relationships and take decisive action to remove yourself from a position of vulnerability. It is however vital that there is a wider reach here and that it will increase vigilance in friends, families or colleagues. The onus to address domestic abuse cannot simply be on the victim. There needs to be collective responsibility for increased awareness. Victims of domestic abuse can feel very vulnerable and for various reasons already discussed, may be hesitant to speak out directly. Of course this does not mean we automatically disclose or report any suspicions we may have as this could put the individual in further danger, however offering support to that individual and making them aware of their options could be extremely important to them. This brings us on to the second term, acknowledgement. Acknowledgement in this context is very different to recognition as it alludes to the fact we may actively know what is happening, but do not wish to associate it with domestic abuse. This could be through fear (specifically if we disclose it to somebody else, which can make it real); it could be because we are in denial and do not wish to accept that somebody who we are in an intimate relationship with could behave in this manner; it could be we have been able to excuse the behaviour, or ultimately it may be that victim blaming is evident to such a degree that we believe that we are the problem in the relationship and not our partner. Whilst some domestic abuse can be overtly vitriolic with no attempt to cover up or excuse the behaviour, this is not wholly common. In many instances the abusive behaviour can be followed by apologies, explanations excusing the behaviour or even victim blaming which attempts to absolve the perpetrator of any wrongdoing. Any of the aforementioned can influence the victim as to whether they acknowledge that they are part of an abusive relationship or whether they are able to justify each instance of abusive behaviour and attribute it to something else. Remember sometimes it can be painful for somebody to accept they may be in a vulnerable position. I have worked with numerous clients whom have directed anger inwardly due to 'allowing themselves' to be in a situation where they have been victims of domestic abuse. Acknowledging and exploring this through therapy can been an extremely emotionally draining experience, not only because you are reliving some unpleasant and emotionally challenging moments, but also because you may then be faced with internalised anger, guilt and self-reproach. These feelings can be powerful and difficult to deal with and therefore in the interest of self-preservation, it is quite common for people not to acknowledge they may be a victim or have any vulnerability.

Whilst we have established some valuable and insightful data around male domestic abuse, what we are not able to do is quantify the true prevalence, which leaves us effectively approximating the real extent of the problem. In essence this becomes a cycle of people not reporting abuse because they do not feel the problem is really understood, but true insight into the problem can be made more difficult due to the low levels of disclosure and reporting. If we are to ever address the real nature of the issue then we must raise awareness levels of domestic abuse and make it easier for people to come forward without the fear of repercussions, whether this is from society, authorities or the perpetrator. Whilst we are simply postulating figures, we will never be able to ascertain the true extent of male domestic abuse and whether it is more prevalent within society than we realise. As well as making it easier for victims to come forward, we must also work to make it harder for perpetrators to hide, to be able to abuse surreptitiously, therefore going undetected and maintaining control over the victim. We do this by talking about domestic abuse and making sure we are all aligned in our approach; we do this by raising awareness society wide as to what does and does not constitute domestic abuse; we do this by galvanising and developing an approach which represents solidarity not division.

When I originally researched publications pertaining to the subject of male domestic abuse, I was surprised at just how difficult it was to locate anything. Certainly, there are books based around data in other countries (USA for example), but it felt very much like anything which specifically focused on the subject area in the UK was at a premium. I wondered whether this meant that male domestic abuse was so rare that it did not necessitate much literature. Perhaps the figures highlight that predominantly, domestic abuse did indeed involve male perpetrators and female victims, and therefore justifiably, the awareness around this subject area needed to focus on highlighting and combatting domestic abuse towards women and girls. We have already identified how many shelters and charities are set up to support female victims and how government strategies (VAWG) have specifically targeted raising the profile of, and supporting female domestic abuse victims. During the research I read an article on the VAWG strategy from a Council (who I shall not name), who spoke about not wishing to exclude boys and men as victims, but highlighted that they felt the evidence substantiated the view it was a gender based crime and that women were disproportionately victims. They estimated that only 30% of domestic abuse victims were male and this explained the gendered approach. If we put that 30% into perspective, the Crime Survey for England and Wales (CSEW) estimated that for the year ending March 2020 approximately 757,000 men aged 16 to 74 years had experienced domestic abuse in the previous year. (This is a prevalence rate of approximately 4 in 100 men)[52]. This raises a question of whether those circa three quarters of a million male domestic abuse victims have a voice. Does minority mean irrelevance? The fact that men feel underrepresented when it comes to tackling domestic abuse means that there is always the capacity for people to become frustrated that the perception appears weighted towards male aggressors and female victims. This has a tendency to create a division between genders and detracts from the real issue which is tackling domestic abuse. The fact that there is a need for publications around male domestic abuse in the first place just serves to highlight the problem. The agenda society wide must not be to tackle female domestic abuse or male domestic abuse. Whilst I applaud different regions having different strategies and clearly some regions have more prevalence than others, there needs to be a national strategy to tackle the issue on a macro level. Disproportionate statistics should not give rise to a focus on one specific area. They should instead highlight that the problem is more widespread. On a global level, we do not have a problem with female domestic abuse and we do not have a problem with male domestic abuse. We have a problem with **domestic abuse** and must refrain from such a myopic view if we are to move forward and try to address this. One of the most difficult challenges we face is the disparity between experiencing domestic abuse and reporting it. This is arguably intrinsically linked with the significant differences between cases reported and cases prosecuted. Of course we are speculating here, however it may be no coincidence that low prosecution rates may dissuade people from coming forward. If you are genuinely in fear of the person you live with then you may experience extreme trepidation reporting the abuse if you feel there is likelihood they will not be reprimanded. The thought of further antagonising that person is often enough for people to suffer in silence. It's imperative we do everything we can to allow those people to find their voice, knowing they do not have to accept what is happening to them and that they will be believed and supported. When people do have the courage to come forward and report domestic abuse, the police must enter that situation open minded, without preconceived ideas or even prejudices. We must move away from men avoiding reporting domestic abuse through fear of counter-allegations and subsequent arrest; We must move away from men fearing ridicule if they are to report being the victims of domestic abuse; We must move away from a societal view that men are not susceptible to domestic abuse because they are perceived to be the stronger sex; and we must move away from society labelling female victims as vulnerable and male victims as weak. If we are to combat domestic abuse holistically, it is imperative we tackle the stigma and perceptions within society in the first instance to remove the gender division. We must galvanise and raise awareness of how to be more vigilant for signs of abuse whether these are physical or emotional. Understanding the right questions to ask and the support available, to provide victims with reassurance they are not alone in facing this, is essential. The truth is we do not know how prominent male domestic abuse is because as we have discussed throughout this book, there are factors which will not only determine how reports are recorded, but whether or not a disclosure is actually made in the first place. In my years as a practicing Psychotherapist I have worked with many abuse victims, both male and female, and seen first-hand the devastating effects this can have on a person and indeed a family. Perhaps the most interesting part, which after reading this book may not come as a surprise to you, is the fact in most cases the client has been unaware they have been the victim of domestic abuse. As I have previously disclosed, whilst I have worked with many abuse victims, never have I worked with somebody who has reported this. In some cases the individual has still been involved in an abusive relationship and has used therapy to address the trauma and explore their options. Some of course feel like their options are limited and use therapy more as a safe space where they can be vulnerable without fear of judgment or consequences.

I don't believe there is an agenda to minimise male domestic abuse, but I do feel some of the information out there and some of the messages pedalled have the potential to be interpreted as quite incendiary. Narratives which purport that domestic abuse carried out by men is more severe and has a greater impact than domestic abuse involving male victims is one that I feel is particularly unhelpful and potentially inflammatory. When I read that women are more likely to experience greater levels of fear, I wonder how such statements are quantified or substantiated. I wonder how it is possible for fear to be a comparatively measurable concept. If male domestic abuse is under-reported, if we do not have an insight into its true prevalence, if we are unaware of its true impact, then how are we able to ascertain whether it is any more or less severe than when it involves female victims? Some of the worst cases of domestic abuse I have personally worked with have involved male victims, people who have been dealing with the emotional fallout many years on. Even if there was substantive evidence which suggested that domestic abuse involving male aggressors does tend to be more severe, we are still left with ambiguity. There is a clear distinction between the act and the impact and quantifying the impact is extremely difficult to do. There lies another difficulty within this narrative, which has the potential to omit an entire community, the LGBT+ community. When we talk about severity of abusive actions being greater with male aggressors, what appears to be taken for granted is the gender of the victim. The automatic assumption and the focus centres round the victim being female. We know this because this rhetoric is found mainly in groups and charities which specifically operate to support female domestic abuse victims. If domestic abuse carried out by males is in fact more severe than abuse carried out by a female counterpart, why does there appear to be a lack of focus on male victims in a same sex relationship? If we then switch the focus to the impact on the victim as opposed to the gender of the aggressor what we are then faced with is an assumption that the physical or emotional impact felt by a female victim is somewhat lessened if the perpetrator is female. So potentially we are left with a question of whether the level of emotional scarring from being subjected to things such as emotional abuse, controlling or coercive behaviour, gaslighting or even physical assault are significantly decreased if the perpetrator is female? In my time practicing psychotherapy, I have not noted a discernible difference between the emotional impact experienced by male and female abuse victims.

There is an argument that in many instances the deepest scars left by domestic abuse are not in fact visible. Any type of abuse can leave us with attachment injury which can have a very profound impact on how we formulate and manage relationships. This can affect all types of interpersonal relationships whether with professional colleagues, friends, family members or a partner. Some may be left with a vulnerability due to low self-esteem and confidence, which leaves them susceptible to abuse in the future. We can be left with a great deal of self-doubt and this can leave us open to falling victim to future abuse if we encounter somebody who can use this to their benefit. Others may experience a very different outlook, having a reticence to trust people, which can leave them closed off emotionally. Such can be that trepidation around trusting people through fear of becoming vulnerable, that relationships with colleagues at work, with family members and even friends can present challenges. A heightened vigilance which perhaps borders on suspicion can also have very serious effects on any future relationships due to the very core foundation of trust and transparency being questioned. Only in recent years have we begun to realise that emotional healing can take significantly longer than physical healing. It is as recently as 2015 that as a society we decided that being controlled or coerced in a relationship was damaging and should not be tolerated. The first female convicted of this crime was in 2018 (Jordan Worth – girlfriend of Alex Skeel, mentioned at the beginning of the book). I must reiterate what must be avoided at all costs, and what has the potential to create friction, is highlighting one cause at the expense of another. We cannot run the risk of female victims being targeted or victimised by people who feel that male victims are overlooked. This detracts from the issue and completely fails at addressing the point. Victims are already reluctant to speak out due to fear of their partner. We cannot exacerbate this with an additional fear of how other areas of society may view or even judge them. The primary aim of all of us working to address this issue has to be to break down barriers, not build them. Ultimately we need to remove as many obstacles as we can which have been preventing people from having the confidence to speak out about being victims of domestic abuse. If we continue with this gendered approach, my fear is that we are putting more obstacles in the way and there is a very real danger of creating resentment between genders, something which is counterproductive.

It is vital that as a society we galvanise and tackle this issue to make it easier to detect, easier to report, easier to move away from, and harder to perpetrate. We must strive for equality in how male victims and female victims are perceived. Domestic abuse has the potential to have cataclysmic effects either physically or emotionally, and whilst the evidence based around reported cases does highlight that a larger percentage of victims are female, it does not mean we should overlook male victims or that their abuse is any less severe or valid. I have worked with men who have been deprived of seeing their children, been ridiculed on social media and have been isolated from friends and family leaving them with nowhere to go, nobody to turn to. Some of these men remained in relationships for years being subjected to this abusive behaviour, feeling isolated due to being alienated from their support network. Whether cases like these involve male or female victims, the emotional consequences can be equally as damaging. The way we handle this is not determined by our gender, it is determined by us as individuals, and how readily we are able to identify and locate our coping strategies, our support network.

We can argue that one of the first things we need to do to address the perception of domestic abuse victims is to provide more awareness about what domestic abuse actually is. Again let us remember that historically domestic abuse was associated with physical violence and the view of the male and female gender within society, perhaps gave rise to the perception that it was a male perpetrated crime. One of the difficulties we have is maintaining that balance between placing the focus on the victims and placing the focus on the abuser. We will always naturally gravitate towards the plight of the victim, and justifiably so, however it is vital we do not completely overlook the circumstances surrounding the perpetrator. Prevention is always preferable to cure and for any successful intervention, we must try to understand what gives rise to the abuse in the first place and tackle these problems at the core.

Domestic abuse has evolved and what falls under this umbrella has grown exponentially. We must accept that both men and women can display violent, manipulative and vindictive tendencies. We must also accept that both men and women can display vulnerabilities and become susceptible to abuse. Once we are able to look at each case in accordance with the specific set of circumstances, to remove gender preconceptions, only then can we begin to tackle domestic abuse as a whole, and not as a gender specific crime.

The case of Jack (see case studies) has implications which reach far beyond he and his family. After all, it will not be recorded as an instance of male domestic abuse; no prosecution depicting the actual events will occur. It will instead likely be viewed as a male perpetrator being acquitted, adding to the statistics of female complainants who do not see charges brought against the accused. Cases like this risk a further societal divide with female campaigners believing that male prosecutions are disproportionate to the number of crimes involving domestic abuse which have been reported by women. On the other hand, campaigners advocating for more recognition for male victims will believe this is just another instance of assumed guilt due to gender, further propagating the view that when it comes to domestic abuse, the default position is that the man will always be the perpetrator and the woman the victim.

If we are to address this, we must remove gender from our

perspective and focus solely on the crime itself. We must allow ourselves to remain objective and discard any preconceived ideas. Whilst ever there exists a conflict between causes each claiming injustice, we remove the focus from what really matters...tackling domestic abuse. We risk channelling the frustration, the anger, the feelings of injustice into the wrong areas and this in turn leaves us in danger of failing to recognise the victims, the vulnerable, the people who need a society working in conjunction, not antagonistically.

11

∾

Case studies

The following case studies are real life accounts of male victims sharing their experiences of being subjected to domestic abuse. Whilst names may have been changed to protect the identity of the individuals and ensure anonymity, their stories are very real.

Each case study involved an in person or online semi-structured interview, which invited each individual to tell their story, to share their experience. All information contained in the following case studies is an accurate reflection of the interviews and does not contain any personal opinion or hypothesis. Any quotes were taken directly from the individual and not amended in any way.

Mark's story

Mark met with me to tell his own personal story of enduring domestic abuse. I sit opposite him, with the emotional effects of recounting his story palpable. At the time Mark was in his late 20's and had a son on the way with his ex-partner. He reflects on his emotional state during this period and how these feelings were exacerbated by an experience he was about to encounter which he says he could never have envisaged.

"It began by just talking online. She intimated to me that her current relationship was violent and abusive. Then one day I just received a message saying she had been locked in the house and had to get out. What else could I do? I had no reason to mistrust her, so irrespective of only having met once in person, I went to collect her and moved her into my house"

Mark went on to say that even though they had only met once previously, they had got on well and there was no indication of anything being untoward. He hadn't hesitated to act in the manner he did because at this time he thought she was in serious danger and he could support her by removing her from the situation.

I asked Mark when he first started to notice any problems within the relationship. He explained to me that in the first couple of weeks, almost daily, her ex-partner had been in touch with him advising him she had been making things up and was lying to him. However, at this stage Mark chose not to believe the things he was hearing, instead feeling that her ex-partner was attempting to deflect from his abusive behaviour.

"Due to my history of mental health I could be impulsive. I believed she was genuine and didn't want her to be in that situation she was describing to me".

Around 2 months into the relationship is when Mark noticed things really started to change. Other people were telling Mark a very different story to the one which he had been led to believe was true. Suddenly he was faced with several people conveying to him occasions when she had been unfaithful, which ultimately she admitted to. Three months into the relationship and things turned physical when Mark had a door kicked in his face off the back of an argument. It was here he began to see a very different side to someone whom at the time he thought he genuinely loved.

"In another heated argument she said she would find where my family were and would cut their throats. Not wishing to fuel the fire and in shock, I backed off, but she reminded me often that if I put a foot wrong she had people on her side such as doormen who she would tell I had raped her and beaten her up".

At this point, Mark became genuinely fearful of the situation he found himself in. He however says he felt embarrassed and ashamed that this was happening to him. As a result he didn't openly disclose to anybody. Mark also says he felt like she deliberately isolated him from friends and family.

"I had been led to believe she was on contraception, yet twice she told me she had been pregnant with my child and then subse-

*quently lost it. Looking back I feel this was part of her desire to
isolate me and convince me I didn't need to see my son, that she
was the only family I needed. Interestingly both of these occasions
came off the back of an argument"*

Mark says he became scared of her, not only physically, but also because of information surrounding her background which he had been made aware of. Many of the threats were subtle, but Mark says he was aware of the undertone when these threats were made.

"She manipulated me into thinking she was the only person I could trust. The abuse started to feel like the norm and within the environment I worked in, I feel there was no way I could have disclosed to anybody."

Ultimately Mark had to leave his job as his partner told the owners he had been domestically abusive towards her. At this point he recollects his self-esteem was extremely low and in arguments she would say very personal and hurtful things to try and belittle him and make him think he was at fault for the problems within the relationship. I asked Mark what support he had at the time, and he said it was only retrospectively that he realised it had been an abusive relationship. He had dismissed the outbursts and tried to rationalise them in the moment. With this in mind he didn't seek any support. He recalls he had told his parents snippets of what had happened but had felt ashamed. Mark ultimately glossed over what was really happening so the individuals he did disclose to received a diluted version of real events.

Sadly, for several reasons, this is not uncommon in cases of abusive relationships.

Mark wanted to tell his story to promote awareness around domestic abuse, mainly to help people recognise the signs and give them hope that you don't have to accept the situation. Talking about telling his story Mark says...

"If one person can become aware and it helps them to identify they are in a relationship which may be abusive and subsequently get out of it, it's job done."

He feels when it comes to domestic abuse the talk is heavily weighted toward violence, but actually this isn't always the most damaging part of abuse.

"The manipulation and controlling side can be just as damaging psychologically with the after effects. This can impact future relationships."

Mark's abusive partner eventually left him for one of the individuals she had been having an affair with. The physical scars have healed, but the psychological ones remain.

"14 years on and there are still occasions whereby I flinch if my wife goes to touch me" he says.

Darren's story

When sitting with Darren, the first thing I note is the change in body language when he begins to talk about his experience. The confident manner he presented upon arrival is suddenly replaced with a range of emotions and you can see some of the pain as he recalls his experience. Darren openly admits that originally he felt that domestic abuse within relationships only manifested itself in the form of domestic violence; more specifically violence with men as the aggressor and women as the victims.

It becomes clear as the interview progresses, that Darren didn't realise the extent of the abuse he was subjected to in his previous relationship. It was only after the relationship had ended that Darren was one day reading an article which highlighted the different forms of abuse, whilst also conveying the fact that men could be victims and were not always perpetrators. Years after this, whilst speaking to a therapist about the subject, Darren realised he too had been a victim of controlling and isolating behaviour. The relationship lasted for around 10 years, but Darren explains, upon reflection it wasn't always bad and the first 3 years showed no warning signs as to what would occur.

"I never realised at the time I was in a domestically abusive relationship. It was only retrospectively that I realised what I had been subjected to. The first 3 years of the relationship upon reflection were in general without too many problems. So what I mean by this is some of the behaviours I became aware of retrospectively, were not evident during those first 3 years."

Darren talks freely about how his ex-partner used methods to try and isolate him from his family.

"Whilst my family never really took to her, I thought it was mainly down to the age difference"

Darren opens up about how her subtle actions whenever his family visited made the environment uncomfortable. He says her inhospitality and the fact she became distant from his family resulted ultimately in them saying they could no longer visit the house if she was present.

"I knew the things she was doing were wrong, but I placated her in fear of the backlash. She was very manipulative and controlling."

The extent of the impact on Darren's family was highlighted when he felt he could no longer attend a family tradition due to the reaction of his partner.

"There was a family tradition where the siblings would gather and have an evening together once every few months. My partner grew jealous of this continuously initiating an argument around why she wasn't invited. Her demeanour made me feel like I was doing something wrong, that it was my fault and I was doing something I shouldn't. Eventually I ceased going to the gatherings."

He felt his family were pulling away from him and these feelings were exacerbated by his partner. When he was having a difficult time, she would tell him that his family didn't care, that they wouldn't come if he needed them, that they would walk down the street and continue right past his house in his time of need. Whilst Darren openly states there were no warning signs in the first 3 years of the relationship, this changed in 2005, when he says he became aware he wasn't happy, but didn't feel he could approach his partner to discuss his feelings and concerns. Some of these concerns were raised through his family who began to disclose some negative things his partner had said and done, which she categorically denied. Whilst Darren says this left him feeling torn and conflicted, he decided to take the word of his partner.

"Ultimately she persuaded me to believe her version of events and the relationship with my family became fraught."

When the feelings of doubt became stronger and more frequent, Darren decided to put the wedding on hold, which he feels was the catalyst for her controlling behaviour. It was at this point he feels the relationship and his partner really began to change. The realisation of the extent of emotional neglect came when Darren was at his lowest point.

"I told her I had just fallen off the bridge and her response was that she couldn't deal with it right now and was taking the kids away for a holiday. I had had traumatic incidents in my job, which had impacted me significantly. I then had a period of physical illness which was quite serious and again I was told my family did not care and they should be knocking on the door to support me. She said it wasn't her job and when I was struggling

with noise she would allow my daughter to scream persistently without attending to her, something she would never usually do."

Darren goes on to say he doesn't feel like the emotional control ended with isolating him from his family. He believed that ultimately, she was also trying to isolate him from his friends too. One of his hobbies was playing on a games console online, with a group of friends. Darren talks about how this was his downtime, his way of relaxing after working in an extremely challenging and highly emotive environment. His partner didn't like him having this time to himself and began to make comments to such an extent that Darren effectively removed himself from socialising with his friends. This didn't go unnoticed and his friends began to comment that he was becoming withdrawn from them.

"Some of my friends began to comment and I felt embarrassed, but I still placated her as I did not want to find out what may happen if I didn't. I really wanted the relationship to work, so didn't want to listen to what others were telling me or take notice of what I had seen from myself."

Darren recalls several pivotal moments upon reflection which ultimately led to him leaving the relationship which for several years had seen him subjected to emotional and psychological abuse as well as controlling behaviour.

Perhaps the most prominent of these was the deception which led to the birth of his 2 children. Darren clearly adores his children, but states there had been no definitive conversation with his partner about conceiving.

"Sex had been intermittent and I had always been led to believe my partner was on the contraceptive pill. Whilst I was aware she wanted children, we had never specifically discussed having them. When she fell pregnant with our first child, I discovered she had not been on any form of contraception. I was warned by a family member that she had deliberately trapped me and would potentially do it again."

Several years later this did indeed happen again when Darren's partner fell pregnant with their second child.

"Suddenly sex between us increased significantly, and what I hadn't realised at the time was that she had again ceased taking the contraceptive pill. This only became evident once she fell pregnant again."

At this point you can see the angst these memories are causing Darren as the realisation of the extent to which he was subjected to controlling behaviour becomes apparent. Recounting the events is clearly extremely painful and traumatic for Darren.

"I felt disgusted, abused and like I had been violated. I should have taken some personal responsibility to be more cautious, but to deceive somebody about taking the contraceptive pill and hide that fact was deplorable."

In 2010 Darren saw further evidence of his partner's abusive behaviour whilst at the wedding of a relative. Due to an injury, Darren was on crutches and was struggling with mobility.

Whilst sitting at the dinner table, at the reception, one of his children was running around at the opposite end of the room. His partner sat there with the expectation of him to go and get her, regardless of his condition. When a family member questioned her regarding this, she became abusive and responded physically.

"Whilst I had a friend constantly highlighting the relationship was toxic, and I knew this, I couldn't physically see a way out. I didn't want to split up my family. It got to a point where I would tell her I was going to work for a long shift and would instead go to a friend's house to talk and do some of the things I didn't feel I was permitted to do at home."

Sadly, things were to get worse for Darren and his low moods became darker and more frequent. He recalls feeling suicidal and desperately wanting the support and reassurance of his partner, but says she simply asked him to leave and go and take some time out to get perspective. Eventually Darren left, walking away with nothing and spending the best part of a year staying on friends' sofas.

Whilst retrospectively he acknowledges he had a lucky escape, at the time, irrespective of all of the warning signs, Darren really struggled emotionally with the breakdown of his relationship. This perhaps substantiates the fact he was oblivious to the controlling and abusive behaviour of his partner, something he is certainly not alone in. Whilst this happened several years ago, Darren still feels the impact.

"I have become averse to intimacy with my wife. I fear I asso-

ciate intimacy with entrapment and this in turn has led to me being distant and emotionally detached" he discloses.

The first thing to understand about Johnny's story is that it is told to me by somebody who was incredibly close to him, to the extent she referred to him throughout as a 'little brother', such was their bond. Tragically in November 2014 aged just 22, Johnny lost his life. His story is one of deep sadness involving physical and psychological abuse, of which it is suspected by his family, ultimately led to his untimely death.

Kirsty remembers vividly receiving the phone call in November 2014, which left her screaming with grief and unable to stop.

"She really did it didn't she?"

These were the first words Kirsty was able to mutter once she had been able to process what she was hearing. These words are extremely powerful and highlight the thought process of somebody who had gradually seen more signs of prolonged abuse on a loved one. We have already explored several different forms of domestic abuse and established for various reasons, some forms can be more diplomatic than others. Sometimes we don't always become aware of the full extent, until we are reflecting, in some cases years on. Tragically, this is one of those occasions.

Kirsty recalls how she was best friends with Johnny's sister growing up and as a result had become extremely close to him. One of the first things she says to me was that he was like the little brother she never had. As a child it transpired Johnny along with his siblings had been subjected to unspeakable molestation from a family member, which had resulted in a very troubled childhood and Kirsty feels, left him vulnerable to predators.

This had impacted him to such a degree that he had made more than one attempt on his own life throughout his teenage years.

Kirsty spoke in detail about the friendship with Johnny, which had begun at a young age.

"We grew up in the 'pines' and Johnny spent all of his free time in the woods. He was a real outdoor person and summer or winter, he would hang out in the woods. He was at his happiest in the woods".

At 16, Johnny was introduced by a friend to a woman. Johnny (then 18) subsequently met the woman's daughter who at the time was 40. They would go on to cohabit before marrying.

A couple of years in Kirsty started to feel like something wasn't quite right in the relationship. She recalls that around 2011, Johnny stopped visiting people as much and when he did come around; his wife would harass him by calling him continuously and screaming at him down the phone.

"When he wasn't with her, that's when she would go completely off the rails, and even if he was with family, she would accuse him of wanting somebody else, or looking at other people"

Kirsty recalls that it didn't take long for her to confirm her suspicions that something really wasn't right in the relationship, and over time began to observe enough signs to suspect Johnny was being subjected to domestic abuse.

"As time went on I could see the abuse that was coming from

her. She would belittle and degrade and constantly harass him. Through this continuous harassment she cost him pretty much every job he had."

Kirsty speaks about Johnny with great fondness and you can see the profound effect his death and the circumstances surrounding it have had on her and the rest of the family. She explains that she had always been there for him and was the first person he would contact if he ever needed anything. Kirsty recalls when she witnessed the abuse first hand, but perhaps even at that time, did not realise the severity and how it would escalate. Johnny had invited her over to cook a meal for her.

"He wanted to give something back to me, as I had always done so much for him"

Kirsty recalls that his wife would continuously pull him away from her and 'berate' him to the extent where the meal was ruined. She says it felt like Johnny's wife did not want him to have any time with her and wanted to be in control of the situation.

The extent of the abuse both physical and psychological would not become apparent until after his death in November 2014. Johnny was found with a fatal knife wound to the chest. It was later discovered that his body was covered with bruises, scratches and burns and raised the question as to whether Johnny had been subjected to lengthy abuse which nobody had ever really known the true extent of. At the time of his death, Kirsty tells me that his wife had been due in court on an assault charge for trying to run Johnny over in her car.

Kirsty and her family have struggled to find any sort of closure as they feel the circumstances around his death raise questions, and those questions to date have never been answered. She struggles with guilt, questioning if there was anything more she could have done to save him. She also feels anger towards the authorities for the way they have viewed his death and spoke about what she perceives to be anomalies in how the death was recorded and the coroner's report. We discussed whether it feels like there is a disparity when it comes to the perception of male domestic abuse and homicide at the hands of a female aggressor. Kirsty says she feels like the police didn't really look into the whole of the circumstances surrounding his relationship and this has left the family feeling angry and with more questions than answers

"They looked at him like he was a troubled individual who had twice tried to hang himself as a young teen". I know if he had have had any of these thoughts he would have spoken to me because I was the one person who was closest to him and he knew was there 24/7. Domestic abuse whether it is on women or men has the potential for lethality. Eventually the emotional or psychological abuse can escalate to physical violence in some form"

The emotion in Kirsty's voice and the expression on her face tells you how much Johnny's suffering, and ultimately his death, have impacted the family and close friends. Kirsty explains that Johnny was about to receive certification to become a professional welder, something which he was both passionate and excited about. She believes that during their friendship, even though he was younger, Johnny had taught her as much as she had taught him. She says the family have been left absolutely devastated and seeking answers which they may never get, and even 6 years on, the pain appears raw.

Kirsty tells me that Johnny's mother still has a very difficult time trying to process the grief surrounding the loss of her youngest son. She does not realise perhaps the true extent of the abuse he was subjected to over the years.

"He was the baby of the family, the glue that held the family together. Now the family is fragmented".

Since Johnny's death, Kirsty has become more vocal about domestic violence and speaking out. She tells me more people who she knows are now coming forward and disclosing about their individual situations. Kirsty actively visits social media platforms to share Johnny's story and encourage men to speak out if they are currently, or have in the past, been the victim of domestic abuse.

"Several male friends have come forward to disclose that they have been subjected to domestic abuse"

Johnny's story is immersed in suffering and tragedy and sadly is not unique. It highlights a very real issue we have with male domestic abuse and perhaps goes further to suggest that a less gendered approach will minimise the stigma and encourage more male victims to speak out.

Toby's story

Toby was just 14 when he first experienced abuse, having struggled to understand his sexuality and reflecting that at the time he was a vulnerable young man. At 16 he left home and begun dating a man 18 years his senior, someone who had experienced sexual abuse himself in his childhood. Whilst at the time, Toby didn't feel like anything untoward was happening, when he talks about the experience now as a 32-year-old man, he believes that there was emotional abuse throughout the relationship.

Toby recalls that his partner had somebody he had previously been romantically involved with, playing a very prominent role in their relationship, something Toby did not question. The relationship in itself lasted for a year, however Toby had moved in with this person after just 3 months, still just 16. He believes that the abuse really began at this point and living with his partner highlighted a very different side to him, something which had not been evident when they had simply been dating.

"The dating period was great, it was when we moved in together that things really begun to change. This was a visible and tangible change where he went from this person who I saw as warmth and safety to something cold and calculating"

Toby highlights that there was infidelity throughout the relationship and recalls the emotional impact this had on him. He feels he became dependent on his partner as he had moved away from his family and was still at a very young age. Toby firmly believes he rapidly went into 'victim mode', which further highlighted his vulnerability. As well as the emotional abuse, he identified that he now knows his partner was also guilty of both controlling and coercive behaviour.

"He did things to try and isolate me from my family."

Toby was subjected to what he described as a 'stream of derogatory comments' about his physical appearance, which he says ultimately resulted in him developing an eating disorder. As well as the overt verbal comments, he feels that there was evidence of more subtle emotional abuse when his partner would often take the side of whom he referred to as 'the third person in the relationship' (his partner's former lover). Toby believes this was done for a very deliberate reason, to make him further question himself and become more dependent.

"The things he was doing eroded my confidence and sense of self until I became subservient to everything he wanted me to do and everything he wanted me to be. I became the 'typical example' of an abuse victim, unable to stand up for myself"

The situation worsened for Toby, and his self-worth, confidence and even his own comprehension of what was happening were questioned, through gaslighting. Toby recalls whilst this began as something quite subtle, it soon escalated and resulted in him questioning his own sanity. He believes his partner could see his techniques were working and therefore would amplify them to see how far he could push the boundaries.

"The more subservient I became, the less I questioned things,

and the more he picked up on this, the more he would continue the gaslighting"

At this point Toby had been completely isolated from friends and family, only occasionally speaking to his Mum. He spoke about having to do this in private when his partner was not there through fear of the repercussions. With the abuse already having a profound impact on him, he then moved away to another region of the country with his partner and his partner's ex-boyfriend, which at the time he didn't question. Toby wasn't allowed to have any time on his own with this individual, being prohibited from even speaking to him. He says it was at this point when the abuse really escalated and recalls the night when things turned physical. Toby had become frustrated at the situation and had voiced his concerns, which had been met with a horrific physical assault.

"He grabbed me by the throat, put me up against the wall and was punching me repeatedly in the face. It was just pure rage and was absolutely terrifying"

Toby recalls his partner approaching him shortly afterwards, quite contritely, offering an olive branch, yet without apologising. He had tried to make a joke of it, but also shift the responsibility onto Toby for speaking to him in a manner which nobody had spoken to him before. Toby firmly believes that the assault had been more attributed to the fact his partner had felt his control slipping and his authority being questioned.

"I knew I had to get out before he killed me"

Toby began to fear for his life and realised that his only option was to flee for his safety. He contacted his Mum who provided him with an excuse and he left the house and never looked back.

"It was like I just left that part of my life right there and walked away from the abuse"

Whilst Toby was able to flee the domestically abusive environment he was in, he feels like the impact followed him into relationships and he spent several years actively pursuing older men who were similar to his ex-partner in several areas. He believes he was very much in love with his ex-partner and wanted to find somebody who would share some of the good qualities he had displayed when the relationship was in its infancy.

However, Toby felt that these relationships were not on the whole healthy due to the intrinsic differences between him as a young adult and partners in their 50's.

"People who have been in abusive relationships can continue to make the same bad choices, actively seeking out people who share characteristics with their former abusers because they don't feel like they deserve anything better."

Toby feels that this pattern could have been avoided for him personally had he had a good level of support around him, somebody to tell him differently. He believes this is sadly an all too typical experience within the LGBT+ community and says that the lack of support means that there is a tendency to latch on to people who may show you attention or display an element of affection towards you.

Toby spent many years suffering from depression as a result of the abuse and still experiences anxiety to this day, some 16 years on from the event. He believes he was vulnerable prior to the relationship and that the abuser was able to quickly identify this and use it to facilitate his abusive behaviour. In subsequent relationships, physical and verbal resemblances to his ex-partner, regardless of intent would be met with him leaving the relationship.

The effects of abuse do not simply end when you are out of the abusive environment, however at that point you have the opportunity to begin to heal and that is what Toby has done over time as he has faced what happened to him.

"Times have changed and support is more readily available through friends and family, but one of the most important things I could say to somebody experiencing what I did, is talk to someone. One of the key factors in abusive behaviour is that isolation. You can break this crucial stage of abuse...talk" he says.

Jack had been in therapy previously where, with his wife (Brenda), it had soon transpired that there were signs of domestic abuse within the relationship. His case contains aspects of emotional, physical and financial abuse as well as gaslighting. Jack describes the relationship in detail from some of the more subtle occurrences to the incident which ultimately proved too much and resulted in him leaving the family home. He says the time between seeking relationship therapy to the time the relationship ended had not been a positive experience and things had not been progressing. Jack highlights there had been a lack of affection and willingness to look at things from a different perspective. He also states there had been a genuine worry around getting a mortgage for the house when the relationship was in trouble, which had caused further friction between them. Reflecting, Jack realised he had been the victim of financial abuse throughout, but hadn't been aware of this at the time.

> *"Everything that I earned was disposable for the family; everything that she earned was hers".*

His monthly salary not only supported the commitments they were jointly responsible for, but also supported his wife Brenda too. Jack explains that he was happy to support Brenda if she did not wish to work, but her deciding to do so was her decision and he respected that. What transpired was something which began as a minor struggle and culminated in Jack becoming financially responsible for all of the household expenditure. It was at this point he realised that his money was for the family, whilst Brenda's was exclusively for her. Arguably for some, this in itself may not present as too much of an issue, but Jack had no control over his money, whether this was money spent on himself, or the purchasing of larger family items. Effectively he was seen as an economic asset. When Jack recounts his story he acknowledges this was the beginning of the abusive behaviour and perhaps also the time when he noticed things begin to escalate with Brenda.

It wasn't just the financial burden which impacted Jack. Sadly he would experience other forms of emotional abuse, which would eventually culminate in domestic violence. He goes on to describe the expectations on him around the house, irrespective of Brenda working shorter hours than he did. Jack was left to do all of the housework, cooking and cleaning and whilst he says he didn't mind taking that time out to do his share, he was ultimately left with no time to himself as the expectation was for him to do everything. He recalls a situation where he asked for help and was met with an abrupt response, which subsequently created a hesitance in approaching Brenda in the future. Jack asked her if she would put the clothes away he had washed and ironed and was met with a curt response.

'Why, I didn't ask you to wash them, so you can put them away yourself.'

Jack proceeds to disclose that looking at the situation retrospectively, he now realises he had been the victim of gaslighting. He disclosed that on one occasion Brenda had told him vehemently that she had cleaned the kitchen, even though he firmly knew she had not. She had actually been baking for herself and

Jack was left to clean the kitchen, but not before doubting himself as to whether she had actually cleaned it like she had professed.

It is important to note, that regardless of the gender of the perpetrator (or victim/survivor) of domestic violence and abuse, it generally does not start out with full violence. Sometimes it is clear, with the benefit of hindsight to see an escalation and where it could eventually end up, but as we have discussed, there are several reasons why we may not recognise this at the time. Jack goes on to describe other incidents, generally each one slightly more inflammatory then the last. It reached a stage where he was unable to leave the house as this would be met with accusations of infidelity.

Jack speaks at length about his experience within this relationship and discloses multiple examples of gaslighting, financial, and emotional abuse. Some of these as isolated incidents may not have generated much suspicion, but considering the frequency and pattern of escalation, they were clearly not conducive to what might be described as a healthy relationship. Jack then reveals the first incident which had led to physical violence. He and Brenda had invited a friend of Brenda's over, who had asked Jack if he would take her to the shops. Jack agreed to do this whilst Brenda remained at home to look after their children as well as the children of her friend. Upon return, the children were found to be unsupervised and immediately Brenda's friend had wanted to contact the police and/or social services. Jack however, was able to reason that there must be a good explanation for Brenda leaving the children alone. At his point Jack admits freely that he didn't wholly believe what he was telling Brenda's friend. It transpired that Brenda had gone to church, and upon her return, Jack had confronted her raising deep concerns over the situation. It was at this stage that Brenda's abuse escalated into physical violence and whilst Jack says he made no attempt to defend himself, he did take the children and leave the house, fearing for their safety. At this stage he began the application for divorce, but wondered whether this was impulsive and withdrew it almost immediately.

The final incident came in 2016 and had a profoundly negative impact on Jack in more than one way. It perhaps also highlights why men can be reluctant to report domestic abuse, and why institutions and public services need to consider the way they handle male domestic abuse reports. Jack recalls that he had had a late night and as a result had decided to stay in bed a while longer the following morning. Ordinarily he says, he would take the children to school on his way to work whilst Brenda slept in, but as it was the school holidays and the children were going into day care at Brenda's place of work, Jack had assumed she would take the children with her when she left. Brenda had become frustrated and shouted at Jack that she didn't want to organise the children and he needed to do it as she was heading off to work. Jack explains he was used to this type of behaviour so got the children ready in preparation to drop them off at Brenda's place of work on his way to his own. Brenda returned some time later seemingly still angry saying she would take the children to work after all. Jack told her to go to work and that as he had already organised them for the day, he would take them. He did admit that his tone may have been provocative at the time, but was ultimately still left in a state of shock at her response.

Brenda started to push Jack and when he did not respond,

begun striking him with a closed fist. Jack says he then pushed her to try and get some space and prevent her from assaulting him further. This seemed to provoke her more and Brenda then began kicking and scratching, as well as continuing the punching. Jack says he tried to calm her down and asked her what she was doing, but there was no reasoning with her and any attempt to defuse the situation was met with further violence. When he managed to restrain her, Brenda bit him and started screaming verbal abuse. Once Jack let her go, she continued the attack, before he was ultimately able to push her away giving him enough time to get the children and lock them all in the bedroom to try and keep safe.

Jack says he was in complete shock and unsure what to do next. He managed to locate his phone and called his boss to explain what had happened. It was his boss who ultimately called the police.

What he hadn't realised is that Brenda had already called the police and what was to follow, only compounded an extremely difficult and emotional situation for him. Four police officers arrived and whilst he was covered in blood scratches and bruises, Jack was immediately cautioned and detained by police. He recalls fearing for the well-being of the children and begged the police not to let the children near Brenda, but was ignored.

It is at this stage of the interview where Jack shows the first glimpse of emotion, describing the shock at being a victim treated as a perpetrator. He says that all the indicators showed he to be the victim, yet this was ignored by the police, who automatically assumed him to be the aggressor. Jack was given a Domestic Violence Protection Order (DVPO), and whilst Brenda was examined, photographs showed no bruising or any broken skin. Jack's trial did not take place until the following year, a wait which had an extremely negative impact on his state of mind, not knowing what would happen and feeling like he was being judged as a perpetrator, when in actuality he was a victim. In addition to this, there was the emotional turmoil at having to leave his children with his wife, wondering what impact the whole situation would have on them. Jack feels like there was a distinct lack of support and even those agencies who were supposed to support him, treated him with suspicion and contempt. It was for this very reason, that he did not file a counter-claim against Brenda. Put simply, he did not feel he was believed and any such allegation, he was warned, could result in the children being taken into care.

Early the following year (after the event), Jack appeared in court charged with Battery (Contrary to Section 39 of the Criminal Justice Act 1988) and Threats to Kill, Contrary to Section 16 of The Offences Against The Persons Act 1861). The evidence was presented almost exactly as described above, yet the trial still went ahead. No witnesses were interviewed that might have heard the shouting or that may have been able to challenge the narrative that Jack was the perpetrator. There were witnesses that had made a video recording of the shouting; these were also not interviewed or questioned. The statement of the first police officer on the scene was not presented into evidence until after the trial had commenced. In her statement the police officer corroborated Jack's account of him being covered in his own blood, yet this was only entered into evidence once the defence lawyer had requested it.

After 2 hours of the second day of the trial the Jury were dismissed to deliberate. The Jury deliberated for 35 minutes to deliver a verdict of not guilty based on the evidence that they both reached out to the police... he had injuries, she had none.

Jack's story is both thought provoking and harrowing. He spent years in an abusive relationship which slowly escalated, culminating in him being the victim of a callous and savage attack. What makes the situation worse is that when he called the authorities for help, he was automatically treated as a perpetrator. It is difficult to ascertain whether this was because his wife was the first to call the police or whether it fits with the narrative of there being an automatic assumption that the male is always the aggressor when it comes to domestic violence. Some welfare agencies have freely admitted they try to emasculate and depower men in these situations, highlighting they are prepared to take the risk that the man may be the victim. Sadly this strategy allows for error when we should be taking a more objective and less assumptive approach to the situation.

As in this instance and many more, it can exacerbate the feelings of powerlessness and being out of control. In essence, the abuse continues, it's just a different perpetrator.

(As told to Eric Hoskins)

Reaching out for help

Mankind

Mankind has been dedicating itself to male domestic abuse victims for 20 years and was the first charity in Great Britain specifically designed to supporting male victims.

Website: https://www.mankind.org.uk

Helpline: 01823 334244

Galop

Galop has been providing support and guidance to the LGBT+ community for over 30 years and specialises in hate crime, domestic abuse and sexual violence.

Website: http://www.galop.org.uk/

Helpine: 0800 999 5428

Men's Aid

Men's Aid has been operating for around 15 years and focuses on alleviating distress and supporting with the emotional and physical wellbeing of male abuse victims.

Website: https://www.mensaid.co.uk/

Helpline: 0333 567 0556

Respect Men's advice line

A confidential advice and support line specifically dedicated to helping male abuse victims. Respect has a range of contact methods which include telephone, e-mail and live webchat.

Website: https://mensadviceline.org.uk

Helpline: 0808 801 0327

Calan DVS

Whilst taking a more holistic approach to tackling domestic abuse, Calan DVS have teams operating across sections of Wales to support male domestic abuse victims.

Website: https://www.calandvs.org.uk

Helpline: 0808 801 0800

AMIS

A charitable organisation which focuses on providing support to male domestic abuse victims in Scotland. AMIS offers confidential support either via e-mail or a national helpline number.

Website: https://abusedmeninscotland.org/

Helpline: 03300 949 395

References

1 Military & Civil

2 Bedfordshire Police (2018) *Abuse victims urged to come forward after landmark court case.* [online] Available at: <https://www.bedfordshire.police.uk/news-and-appeals/jordan-worth-domestic-abuse-apr2018#d9761326>

3 Elkin, M. (2018) *Domestic abuse in England and Wales: year ending March 2018.* Office for National Statistics. [online] Available at: <https://www.ons.gov.uk/peoplepopulationandcommunity/crimeandjustice/bulletins/domesticabuseinenglandandwales/yearendingmarch2018>

4 Stripe, N. (2020) *Domestic abuse victim characteristics, England and Wales: year ending March 2020.* Office for National Statistics. [online] Available at: <https://www.ons.gov.uk/peoplepopulationandcommunity/crimeandjustice/articles/domesticabusevictimcharacteristicsenglandandwales/yearendingmarch2020#sex>

5 National Archives (2021) *Living in 1901 – Women's Work.* [online] Available at: <http://www.nationalarchives.gov.uk/pathways/census/living/making/women.htm>

6 Roantree, B. & Vira, K. (N.D.) *The rise and rise of women's employment in the UK.* IFS Briefing Note BN234. [online] Available at: <https://www.ifs.org.uk/uploads/BN234.pdf>

7 Evans, M. (2016) How male victims of domestic abuse often end up getting arrested themselves. *The Telegraph* [online] Available at: <https://www.telegraph.co.uk/news/uknews/crime/12061547/How-male-victims-of-domestic-abuse-often-end-up-getting-arrested-themselves.html>

8 Brooks, M. (2018) *Male victims of domestic and partner abuse 35 key facts.* Mankind [online]. Available at: <https://www.mankind.org.uk/wp-content/uploads/2018/03/35-Key-Facts-Male-Victims-March-2018.pdf>

9 Elkin, M. (n 3)

10 *Serious Crimes Act 2015* [online] London: The Stationery Office. Available at:
   <https://www.legislation.gov.uk/ukpga/2015/9/section/76/enacted>

11 Home Office (2021) *Review of the Controlling or Coercive Behaviour Offence.* [online] Available at: <https://assets.publishing.service.gov.uk/government/uploads/system/uploads/attachment_data/file/965361/review-of-the-controlling-or-coercive-behaviour-offence-horr122.pdf>

12 Home Office (n 11)

13 Mankind (2021) *Statistics on Male Victims of Domestic Abuse.* [online] Available at: <https://www.mankind.org.uk/statistics/statistics-on-male-victims-of-domestic-abuse/>

14 Mankind (n 13)

15 Home Office & Bradley, K. (2015) *Coercive or controlling behaviour now a crime.* Gov.UK. [online] Available at: <https://www.gov.uk/government/news/coercive-or-controlling-behaviour-now-a-crime>

16 Abbreviation for ending 'violence against women and girls'

17 Campbell, D. (2010) More than 40% of domestic violence victims are male, reports reveals. *The Guardian*. [online] Available at: <https://www.theguardian.com/society/2010/sep/05/men-victims-domestic-violence>

18 Home Office & Atkins, V. (2019) *Government unveils commitments to tackle abuse against men*. Gov.UK. [online] Available at: <https://www.gov.uk/government/news/government-unveils-commitments-to-tackle-abuse-against-men>

19 Rees, J. (2019) Male domestic abuse victims 'suffering in silence'. *BBC News*. [online] Available at: <https://www.bbc.co.uk/news/uk-wales-47252756>

20 Police recorded crime: Home Office

21 Klein, C. (2019). *Stockholm Syndrome: The True Story of Hostages Loyal to Their captors*. [online]
Available at: <https://www.history.com/news/stockholm-syndrome>

22 Elkin, M. (n 3)

23 Elkin, M. (n 3)

24 Doward, J. (2003) Battered men get their own refuge. *The Guardian*. [online] Available at: <https://www.theguardian.com/society/2003/dec/21/socialcare.uknews>

25 Tobin, O. (2018) Charity warning over lack of refuges for male victims of domestic abuse in London. *Evening Standard*. [online] Available at: <https://www.standard.co.uk/news/crime/there-are-no-male-safe-houses-for-male-victims-of-domestic-abuse-in-london-and-a-charity-is-asking-a3912091.html>

26 Brooks, M. (2016) Briefing: Refuges and safe houses for male victims of domestic abuse. Mankind. [online] Available at: <http://new.mankind.org.uk/wp-content/uploads/2015/05/Refuges-for-Male-Victims-of-Domestic-Abuse-Briefing-July-2016.pdf>

27 The Guardian (2016) *Women who bullied husband is jailed for life after murdering him.* [online] Available at: <https://www.theguardian.com/uk-news/2016/mar/08/sharon-edwards-woman-bullied-murdered-husband-jailed-for-life>

28 Dearden, L. (2017) Male rape, harassment and domestic abuse to be tackled by new government drive. *Independent*, [online] Available at:<https://www.independent.co.uk/news/uk/home-news/male-rape-sexual-violence-domestic-abuse-violence-against-women-cps-vawg-prosecutors-help-support-a7931956.html>

29 Dearden, L. (n 28)

30 Rape Crisis (2021) *Statistics – sexual violence.* [online] Available at: <https://rapecrisis.org.uk/get-informed/about-sexual-violence/statistics-sexual-violence/>

31 Idriss, M. (2018) *The forgotten male victims of honour-based violence.* The Conversation. [online] Available at: <https://theconversation.com/the-forgotten-male-victims-of-honour-based-violence-96041>

32 Kaur, B. (2019) *'Honour'-Based Violence and Forced Marriage: A Study Guide* [online] Available at: <https://documents.manchester.ac.uk/display.aspx?DocID=42590>

33 Ministry of Justice, Home Office & the Office for National Statistics (2013) *An Overview of Sexual Offending in England and Wales.* [online] Available at <https://assets.publishing.service.gov.uk/government/uploads/system/uploads/attachment_data/file/214970/sexual-offending-overview-jan-2013.pdf>

34 Harmes, L. & Forde, E. (2018) Male stalking victim: 'People don't take you seriously'. *BBC News*. [online] Available at: <https://www.bbc.co.uk/news/uk-42582820>

35 Greenberg, E. cited in Petric, D (2018) *Gaslighting and the knot theory of mind*. [online] Available at: <https://www.researchgate.net/publication/327944201_Gaslighting_and_the_knot_theory_of_mind>

36 Sarkis, S. (2017) *11 Warning signs of Gaslighting*. [online] Available at: <https://www.psychologytoday.com/us/blog/here-there-and-everywhere/201701/11-warning-signs-gaslighting>

37 McLeod, S. (2016) *Albert Bandura's Social Learning Theory: Simply Psychology* [online] Available at:
<https://www.simplypsychology.org/bandura.html>

38 *Serious Crime Act 2015* (n 10)

39 CPS (2017) *Controlling or Coercive Behaviour in an Intimate or Family Relationship*. [online] Available at: <https://www.cps.gov.uk/legal-guidance/controlling-or-coercive-behaviour-intimate-or-family-relationship>

40 Fiebert, M. & Tucci, L. (1998) Sexual Coercion: Men Victimized by Women. *The Journal of Men's Studies*. 6(2),127-133

41 Brooks, M. (n 8)

42 Postmus, J., Hoge, G., Breckenridge, J., Sharp-Jejjs, N. & Chung, D. (2018) *Economic Abuse as an Invisible Form of Domestic Violence: A multicountry Review*. [online] Available at: <https://www.researchgate.net/publication/324063627_Economic_Abuse_as_an_Invisible_Form_of_Domestic_Violence_A_Multicountry_Review>

43 A UK based charity, which focuses on ending domestic abuse

44 The week (2018) *When did marital rape become a crime?* [online] Available at <https://www.theweek.co.uk/98330/when-did-marital-rape-become-a-crime>

45 Musimbe-Rix, S. (2020) *Research: Domestic Abuse in LGBT Communities*. Kent, Surry & Sussex Community Rehabilitation Company. [online] Available at: <https://www.ksscrc.co.uk/2020/04/30/research-domestic-abuse-in-lgbt-communities/>

46 Haringey London (2017) *Haringey Violence against Women and Girls Partnership: Briefing: Responding to violence against men and boys*. [online] Available at:<https://www.haringey.gov.uk/sites/haringeygovuk/files/men_and_boys_briefing_2017.pdf>

47 Guasp, A. (2011). *Gay and Bisexual Men's Health Survey*. London: Stonewall AND Hunt, R. & Fish, J. (2008) *Prescription for change: Lesbian and bisexual women's health check 2008*. London: Stonewall UK.

48 Magic, J & Kelley, P. (2018) *LGBT+ People's experience of domestic abuse: a report on Galop's domestic abuse advocacy service.* London: Galop

49 Hunte, B. (2020) Lockdown: Suicide fears soar in LGBT community. *BBC News* [online] Available at: <https://www.bbc.co.uk/news/health-53223765>

50 BBC News (2018) *Male Domestic Abuse: Not enough support for victims says charity*. [online] Available at: <https://www.bbc.co.uk/news/uk-england-45490173>

51 Stripe, N. (n 4)

52 *Local Government Act 1988.* London: The Stationery Office. [online] Available at: <https://www.legislation.gov.uk/ukpga/1988/9/contents>

Bibliography

The following references were not cited in text, but are nonetheless credit worthy:

Bullock, C. & Beckson, M. (2011) Male Victims of Sexual Assault: Phenomenology, Psychology, Physiology. *The Journal of the American Academy of Psychiatry and the Law*, 39 (2), 197–205

Citizens Advice Bureau (2014) *Controlling money, controlling lives – Financial abuse in Britain*. [online] Available at: <https://www.citizensadvice.org.uk/Global/Migrated_Documents/corporate/controlling-money-controlling-lives--1-.pdf>

Coxell, A. & King, M. (1996) Male victims of rape and sexual abuse. *Sexual and Relationship Therapy*, 11 (3), 297-308

End the fear (2021) *Same sex domestic abuse*. [online] Available at: <http://www.endthefear.co.uk/same-sex-domestic-abuse/>

Sexual Offences Act 2003. London: The Stationery Office. [online] Available at: <https://www.legislation.gov.uk/ukpga/2003/42/section/1>

Holtzworth-Munroe, A. (2005) Female perpetration of physical aggression against an intimate partner: A controversial new topic of study. *Violence and Victims*, 20, 251–259

Judge, M. (2017) Women Who Emotionally Abuse Men. *Intellectual Takeout*. [online] Available at: <https://www.intellectualtakeout.org/blog/women-who-emotionally-abuse-men/>

Justice, J. (2019) *The Difference Between Emotional and Psychological Abuse.* [online] Available at: <https://www.jaredjustice.com/blog/the-difference-between-emotional-and-psychological-abuse/>

Manchester Safeguarding Partnership (2021) *Coercive control, controlling behaviour & psychological abuse – advice for all.* [online] Available at: <https://www.manchestersafeguardingpartnership.co.uk/resource/psychological-abuse-advice-for-all/>

Mankind (2021) *Statistics and Research.* [online] Available at: <https://www.mankind.org.uk/statistics/>

Mankind (2021) *Types of domestic abuse.* [online] Available at: <https://www.mankind.org.uk/help-for-victims/types-of-domestic-abuse/>

McLean, I., Balding, V. & White, C. (2004) Forensic medical aspects of male-on-male rape and sexual assault in greater Manchester. *Med Sci Law*. 44(2), 165-169

Petric, D. (2018). *Gaslighting and the knot theory of mind.* [online] Available at: <https://www.researchgate.net/publication/327944201_Gaslighting_and_the_knot_theory_of_mind>

Platt, J. & Busby, D. (2009) Male Victims: The Nature and Meaning of Sexual Coercion. *The American Journal of Family Therapy,* 37(3), 217-226

Rahman, G. (2018) *Are a third of domestic abuse victims men?* Full Fact. [online] Available at: <https://fullfact.org/crime/are-third-domestic-abuse-victims-men/>

Relate (2021) *What is emotional abuse?* [online] Available at: <https://www.relate.org.uk/relationship-help/help-relationships/arguing-and-conflict/what-emotional-abuse>

Skentelbery, H. (2020) Special constable jailed for controlling and coercive behaviour. *Warrington Worldwide.* [online] Available at: <https://www.warrington-worldwide.co.uk/2020/01/29/special-constable-jailed-for-controlling-and-coercive-behaviour/>

Snyder, C. (2020) *How to Identify Financial Abuse in a Relationship.* Verywell mind. [online] Available at: <https://www.verywellmind.com/financial-abuse-4155224>

Swerling, G. (2019) Men becoming 'increasing victims' of coercive control, legal experts claim. *The Telegraph.* [online] Available at: <https://www.telegraph.co.uk/news/2019/03/09/men-becoming-increasing-victims-coercive-control-legal-experts/>

The National Archives (2013) *An Overview of Sexual Offending in England and Wales.* [online] Available at: <https://webarchive.nationalarchives.gov.uk/20140711232238/https://www.gov.uk/government/publications/an-overview-of-sexual-offending-in-england-and-wales>

Titchener, N. (2019) *Marital Rape Law in the UK: what is it? Lawtons* Solicitors. [online] Available at: <https://www.lawtonslaw.co.uk/resources/what-are-the-legal-penalties-for-marital-rape/>

Lightning Source UK Ltd.
Milton Keynes UK
UKHW020802180821
389045UK00003B/13